Ghosts of F

Investigating Cowtown's Most Haunted Locations

Brian Righi

Schiffer Publishing Ltd®

4880 Lower Valley Road Atglen, Pennsylvania 19310

Designed by John P. Cheek
Type set in Decaying/News Gothic BT

ISBN: 978-0-7643-2813-8
Printed in China

Published by Schiffer Publishing Ltd.
4880 Lower Valley Road
Atglen, PA 19310
Phone: (610) 593-1777; Fax: (610) 593-2002
E-mail: Info@schifferbooks.com

For the largest selection of fine reference books on this and related sub-jects, please visit our web site at **www.schifferbooks.com**
We are always looking for people to write books on new and related subjects. If you have an idea for a book please contact us at the above address.

This book may be purchased from the publisher.
Include $3.95 for shipping.
Please try your bookstore first.
You may write for a free catalog.

In Europe, Schiffer books are distributed by
Bushwood Books
6 Marksbury Ave.
Kew Gardens
Surrey TW9 4JF England
Phone: 44 (0) 20 8392-8585; Fax: 44 (0) 20 8392-9876
E-mail: info@bushwoodbooks.co.uk
Website: www.bushwoodbooks.co.uk
Free postage in the U.K., Europe; air mail at cost.

Dedication

For Raymond and Patricia Righi, who raised me on the kind of stories that made it hard to sleep at night.

Acknowledgments

Believe it or not this is my favorite part of the whole book, when I can sit back and thank everyone who has helped me in the creation of this work. Writing may take a lot of sitting in front of the computer monitor typing-away, but it's certainly not a solitary endeavor. So without further ado let me thank my editor, Dinah Roseberry, for making this a reality, and Angela Conley for all her love, support, and photographic expertise.

I can also not forget my good friend Robert Larson for always believing in me, nor my ghost hunting pals Carl Hullett, Amy Wainwright, and Barry Turnage from DFW Ghost Hunters for the many wonderful nights together in cold, damp cemeteries freezing our you-know-what's off.

In addition, let me thank all of those who opened their homes and businesses for me to prowl around in, or who were willing to share their stories after I'd nagged them to death.

Finally, to the City of Fort Worth, which inspired these tales—I fondly call you my home.

Contents

Haunted Fort Worth

1. Oakwood Cemetery. 2. Carter Ghost Town. 3. Miss Molly's Bed & Breakfast. 4. Stockyard's Hotel. 5. Swift Building. 6. Log Cabin Village. 7. Peter Brothers Hats. 8. Del Frisco's Steakhouse. 9. Jett Building. 10. Barber's Books. 11. Texas White House. 12. Thistle Hill. 13. Schoonover Mansion. 14. Mistletoe Heights House. 15. Armstrong House. 16. Weslyan Theater. 17. Bird's Fort. 18. "Death's Crossing." 19. "Lost Cemetery of Infants." 20. Veal Station Cemetery.

A Texas Yankee

I came to Fort Worth, Texas by way of the "Windy City" of Chicago, Illinois and from the start my friends joked that I was that "Damn Yankee" who just wouldn't leave. Despite their good-natured ribbing, Fort Worth is a city that I have come to love and cherish... A city filled with enough history and legend to keep any writer busy for the better part of a lifetime.

Fort Worth began as a humble military post named after General William Jenkins Worth in 1849. A hero of the Mexican War, General Worth had proposed a line of forts along the Texas frontier for the protection of settlers on their westward journey. The fact that numerous Indian tribes posed a threat in the area did little to deter hardy pioneers looking for a new life and a little breathing room. Soon settlers began flocking to the little post on the bluffs, overlooking the Trinity River, bringing with them not only their hopes and dreams, but trade and commerce. A general store sprang up, as well as a flourmill, and in time the Southern Pacific Stage Line used it as a stop on its way to California. As the Indian threat diminished, the army moved to another fort, pushing the frontier even farther west and leaving, what was once a small military post in the middle of nowhere, a now thriving community.

Fort Worth fared well until, like much of the south, the effects of the Civil War devastated it in the 1860s. These were bleak times for residents and everything from beans to bars of soap were in short supply. One by one, families began packing up their wagons in search of greener pastures, and the population of the once prosperous town dropped to as few as 175 souls. Gradually, however, Fort Worth began to revive with a much-needed economic shot in the arm from the developing cattle industry. Cowboys weary from cattle drives to Kansas meat markets began referring to this oasis of the prairies as "Cowtown," a moniker many Fort Worth residents to this day proudly claim as their own.

If the cattle trade brought with it a new measure of success, then it also attracted a wide host of colorful characters. Gunfights, saloons, and gambling parlors became common in a dangerous section of town notoriously known as "Hell's Half Acre." Outlaws such as Butch Cassidy and the Sundance Kid and the infamous Sam Bass Gang rode through its streets with impunity. As one early headline read, when describing a local drinking establishment there, "They Raise Merry Cain at the Waco Tap." By 1876, lawlessness was so rampant in this part of town that citizens brought in "Longhaired Jim" Courtright to restore order. In time things would settle down and "Hell's Half Acre" would become the stuff of legend as Fort Worth grew to become what I like to call "a very big little town." Big enough that is, to develop interstates and art galleries, but small enough that you still get a warm smile and a "howdy" from strangers as you pass by.

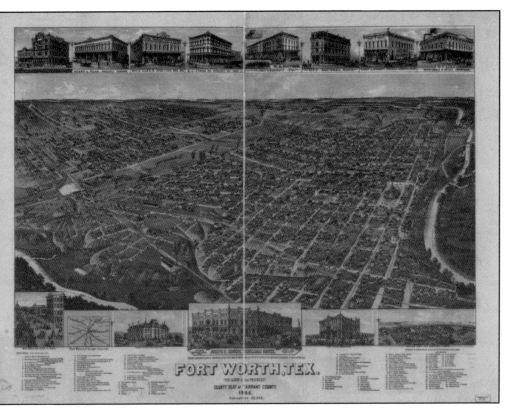

Fort Worth, Texas: "Queen of the Prairies", 1886.
Courtesy of Milwaukee, Norris, Wellge & Co.

In writing this book, two of Fort Worth's greatest qualities became key to its completion. The first is that Fort Worth's citizens love nothing better than a good story. Whether it's a bit of local history or a Texas size tall tale, you can always find someone willing to sit down and spin you a yarn. The second is that the streets here are filled with ghosts. Time and again I listened with rapt attention to the legends of phantoms that haunt its cemeteries or wander its rambling old mansions. As something of a collector of folklore tales, I've always had an affinity for ghost stories—the scarier the better. It was in the hopes of sharing with the reader some of the color and history that made Fort Worth what it is today that I began to seek out and examine its most haunted locations. It's important to remember, however, that each of these stories focuses on more than just dime store novel characters, but on real flesh and blood people like you and I; people who lived lives, raised families, and fought to tame a land. If for nothing else then, they deserve our respect and compassion. So join me if you will, as we begin our journey and examine the 'Ghosts of Cowtown'.

The Lady of
Oakwood Cemetery

*"Show me your cemeteries, and I will tell you
what kind of people you have."*
- Benjamin Franklin

Early on one of the first locations I was determined to investigate was none other than Fort Worth's Oakwood Cemetery, where stories that a figure in white roaming its grounds at night were being reported by those whose homes bordered the property. Some claimed it was a beautiful woman dressed in a bridal gown, calling out to some forgotten lover. Others said that she carried a lantern and wandered aimlessly through the tombstones searching for her lost children. Finally, the stories went as far as to warn that cars passing on the road nearby would sometimes lose power and come to a stop, as if their batteries had been drained. This was one story I just couldn't pass up.

Oakwood Cemetery sits nestled on the gently sloping bluffs above the Trinity River at Grand Avenue and Gould Street on the city's north side. Its sprawling grounds lie shaded in the numerous tall oak trees from which it derives its name and it can be argued by most that it provides one of the best views of Fort Worth's downtown area. Originating as a donation of land by one of its early settlers, John Peter Smith, in 1879, Oakwood is actually

Entrance to Oakwood Cemetery.

comprised of three cemeteries that grew over the years into one large necropolis. The first was simply known as the City Cemetery and was the final resting place for most of the Fort Worth's citizens. The second section was known as Calvary Cemetery and was created for the burial of the city's Catholic population. At the time there were no bridges spanning the Trinity River and funerals held in the downtown parish cathedral would be forced to cross at shallow fords. During heavy rains the river swelled and mourners in the procession would have to turn back while the coffin continued onward. This led to a rather colorful saying: that if a person were a good friend, "they would follow you across the river." The final section of the cemetery was called Trinity Cemetery and was designed for the burial of the city's African Americans, demonstrating that at the time of segregation, it extended to death as well as in life.

Today, city leaders tend to gloss over these differences and proudly claim that Oakwood is: "The final resting place of cattle kings and cotton kings, of oil barons and business tycoons, of bankers and statesmen. There are writers, and musicians, brave soldiers and beautiful women…" (Chapman, 2006, B4). Oakwood is literally the final resting place of the who's who of Fort Worth's history. Even famous lawman "Longhaired Jim" Courtright who helped tame "Hell's Half Acre," now lies quietly beneath its soil after one too many gunfights. But of all the soldiers, scoundrels, and statesmen buried here, it's the phantom of an unknown woman reluctant to leave its grounds that I was hunting after.

When I first pulled up to the wrought iron gates of Oakwood Cemetery sometime after sundown, I couldn't help but notice how different the place looked at night. During the day the grounds are well kept and peaceful, a rather proper place to be buried, but at night it takes on a much more sinister aspect. Gravel paths and inviting lanes of ornate mausoleums are transformed into dark hulking shapes and the once majestic oaks that seem to thrive here now hiss angrily as the wind passed through their branches. Maybe coming here alone at night wasn't such a good idea after all (a big mistake, I would later learn from other ghost hunters). Nevertheless, I puffed up what little courage I had and entered through the large iron gates armed with nothing more than a flashlight and camera. To be honest I kept expecting to see a sign reading, "Abandon All Hope Ye Who Enter Here," but the only ones posted at the time were historical markers proclaiming some of the more famous burials at Oakwood.

Wandering through the maze of statuary and grave markers, snapping pictures in the hopes of capturing the elusive phantom on film, I began to get a better feel for the layout of the place. I also realized just how much an over-active imagination can play on the senses. Believe me, when you're in a cemetery alone at night, you tend to see things out of the corner of your eye and hear the snapping of twigs much louder than before. It was easy to see why people passing by at night might think this a good place for a haunting.

After several hours of exploring, I began to think that the phantom wouldn't show up after all; a fact I was secretly relieved by. I was thinking that perhaps I should just write the whole thing off and chalk it up to urban legend when a low, mournful wail broke the silence. From a dark cluster of oak trees about one hundred yards away, I watched as a figure in white slowly moved in my direction. Now it's hard to say what a person would really do under these circumstances. Would you start snapping pictures like a brave investigator, undeterred by the ghost coming toward you, or would you take to your heels and run like the devil himself were after you? Admittedly I did neither. Instead, I simply froze, and watched the figure lumber closer and closer to my position behind a tombstone. It wasn't until the figure disappeared behind another set of trees and then re-emerged much closer that I recognized what was coming towards me. I wasn't witnessing the famous wailing phantom of Oakwood Cemetery—I was being scared to death by a milk cow that had wandered in to feed on the cemetery's lush grass and belt out an occasional "moo." The fact of the matter struck me as so funny that as soon as I could catch my breath, I began to laugh long and hard. I laughed so hard I scared the poor cow, which immediately tore off through the cemetery in the opposite direction as if it had seen a ghost.

At this point I decided that both the poor cow and I had probably had enough excitement for one evening and started to make my way back to the safety of my waiting car. I couldn't help but wonder though, if the phantom was just waiting for me to leave before resuming her nocturnal wandering, or maybe, just maybe, I had met the phantom of Oakwood Cemetery, and we scared each other to death. Either way Oakwood Cemetery remains a place of stories both night and day, and if you go there listen carefully because you might just hear a few.

Oakwood Cemetery, 701 Grand Avenue, Fort Worth, Texas 76106

The Town that Disappeared

"Any rugged pathway may have the marks
of enchantment."

- H. Bryant Prather,
Gleamings of the West

Following my last adventure in Oakwood Cemetery, I knew I was in need of help and so turned to north Texas's leading experts in ghost hunting, Carl Hullett and Les Ramsdale, with the North Texas Research Society. After contacting them and filling them in on the details of what would later become this book, they readily agreed to introduce me to the lost town of Carter, Texas and, what they called, "a ghost hunter's paradise." Lying on the outskirts of Fort Worth, the long forgotten town of Carter was filled, they claimed, with the paranormal activity of its former ghostly residents.

We began the evening in the parking lot of the local IHOP Restaurant and, after exchanging introductions and checking equipment, we piled into Carl's minivan for the short trip to Carter. Along the way the two found a lot to laugh at when I told them of my experience with the cow in Oakwood Cemetery and to this day Carl still teases me that I should have touched the cow to make sure it was real. Located northwest of Fort Worth down a series of twisting gravely roads that all look the same at night, I was glad that I was in the company of such expert guides. It was obvious that attempting to find the place by myself would have left me completely confused and hopelessly lost. The trip did give me a chance to listen as the two ghost hunters took turns recounting the history of the place. It gave me a better understanding of just what I was in for.

Established in 1866 by three families led by Judge W. F. Carter, for whom the town was named, T. Parkinson, and H. C. Vardy, the early settlement was initially a watering place for thirsty cattle herds needing to rest for the night. Cartersville as it was first known spread itself along the banks of the Clear Fork River and when it was discovered that another town by the same name already existed, the settlers opted to shorten the name to simply Carter. A flourmill was built next to the river as more settlers began arriving and in time the town became famous for the quality of the flour that it produced. Other businesses necessary for a frontier town to survive sprang up, including a gin mill, schoolhouse, church, blacksmith's shop, and general store. By 1888, the town's population reached 75 residents and boasted its very own post office.

Though the town lacked some of the rowdier establishments more common to nearby Fort Worth, like saloons and roadhouses, it was not without its share of drifters and ruffians willing to settle disputes with the barrel of a gun. One such occasion chronicled by local historians involved a man from Carter who began to gossip rather loudly that Old Hamp Good over in the town of Clear Fork was a no good cattle rustler. In an era where cattle rustling was not uncommon and carried with it the hangman's rope, Old Hamp did not take too kindly to the accusation. Late one December night Old Hamp rode into Carter filled with hard liquor and looking for a fight. After exchanging a few angry words with his accuser at the man's home, gunfire broke out between the two. When the bullets stopped flying and the dust finally settled, the accuser lay dead on his porch and Old Hamp made his way back to Clear Fork badly wounded.

All that remains of Carter Ghost Town.

If it wasn't gunfights the early townsfolk had to contend with, then it was the frequent raids from hostile Indians. The town lived under constant threat of attack and during its history several of the town's children were abducted by marauding bands of Indians, never to be heard from again. In one incident during August of 1872, a group of town's men were returning home after an evening of church going in nearby Veal Station. As the shadows along the roadway began to lengthen, gunfire erupted from the bushes on either side. The cry of "ambush" rang out as most of the men made a quick getaway, but Joseph Hemphill's horse was shot out from under him. In the chaos that ensued the attacking Indians sprang from their hiding places, scalping and killing the unfortunate Joseph.

The township of Carter may have survived cattle rustling, gunfights, and Indian raids, but in the end time itself would conspire to finish it off. Eventually the flourmill burned down, businesses closed for lack of customers, people moved away to bigger cities, and when the railroad bypassed it, the town simply disappeared. By the 1920s, there was nothing left of Carter but an old whitewashed church and an adjacent tabernacle sitting in a small glade of evergreen trees surrounded by rolling hills and the sounds of a bubbling creek. That is after all, if you don't count the ghosts said to still haunt the place.

When we arrived Carl and Les began setting up their sound recorders and cameras under the tabernacle as I wandered the deserted glade reading the ten stone historical markers that dotted the area, detailing the events of the town like gravestones. We then hunkered down to take photos and my guides began explaining some of the paranormal activity reported here. Over the years ghost hunters have captured a number of astounding images of bright glowing orbs and floating, ectoplasmic mist that they couldn't account for. Les also took the time to play back an audio recording he took late one night in the old church house of a little girl's voice reciting her ABCs. He also played another audio clip that sounded much like the faint voice of a small boy answering with the word "Booker" when investigators asked aloud the name of the ghost that haunted the old church. But what captivated me more than these eerie voices from the past was another experience Les had in which he believes he walked right through one of Carter's ghostly inhabitants.

During one investigation while photographing a field behind the church he began to feel as if he were being watched. Turning to move to another location, he suddenly felt as if his whole body was being slammed by a bone-chilling electrical shock that passed through him and dissipated as it moved on.

"It was like a block of ice being passed through my body with jumper cables attached to it," he explained.

Other strange occurrences blamed on the ghosts of Carter include uncanny equipment failures that seem to plague many of the ghost hunters that come to here. Fresh batteries are often drained of their charges, while equipment left unattended has appeared and disappeared in different locations unexpectedly. In some cases, electronic monitoring devices used by ghost hunters to track spirit movement are simply turned off by unseen hands.

Carl and Les are convinced that two of the ghosts haunting Carter belong to the playful spirits of children that once lived and died here. Possibly a boy and girl, whose voices they captured on sound recordings and may have been the victims of an Indian raid.

"Whoever they may be they seem more intent on being mischievous than anything else," explained Les. "Who knows, the place could be filled with many more ghosts as well. We just don't know for sure."

Before wrapping up the evening I asked Les to show me the spot in which he encountered the frightening coldness. Only too happy to oblige my curiosity he led me to a vacant spot behind the church.

"There it is," he pointed, and watched as I snapped away a few pictures. "That's where it happened."

Although there wasn't a hint of coolness in the warm, Texas air, and I didn't feel anyone watching me, days later I discovered something strange when examining the photographs from that night. In one, taken from that very spot, was the image of a large, glowing orb with a bright tail moving in a downward motion. I was amazed, to say the least. There were no observable light sources at the time and the orb was not visible to the naked eye.

When I called Les to tell him about the strange object I had captured that night, he simply responded, "Yep, that's Carter for ya."

Was it the image of some child's ghost sneaking up on me to pull a devilish little prank or perhaps the spirit of an early gunfighter who died violently at that spot and was wondering just what I was doing? The answer to this question may never be known, but if some night you happen to navigate your way through the twisting maze of gravel roads and chance upon a small glade with a church and tabernacle, you just may find out for yourself.

Carter Ghost Town: from Springtown travel five miles south on Highway 51; turning west onto Carter Road for approximately one mile.

The Friendly Gals of Miss Molly's

"Street ladies bringing in sailors must pay
for room in advance."
>   - A sign posted outside one of
>   Miss Molly's rooms

Walking down the brick paved streets of Fort Worth's historical stockyard district you can find everything from ten-gallon hats at the Longhorn Trading Company to cold beers at the White Elephant Saloon. What most of the tourists thronging its thoroughfares don't know, however, is that perched above the Lonestar Café sits Miss Molly's, the oldest functioning Bed and Breakfast in the city. A place filled not only with a rather colorful past, but with what some think are the ghosts of its former occupants. Now, with a few investigations under my belt, I felt it was time to pay this quaint little place a visit and learn more about the stories surrounding it.

The stockyards began as a sprawling complex of cattle pens and auction houses in 1893, and soon began to compete with rival markets in Kansas City. Cattle were driven right down Main Street to waiting pens in the stockyards, in a stream of hooves and horns, often forcing pedestrians off the street until they passed. To meet the needs of the cowboys, drummers (traveling salesmen), and cattle buyers who came to do business at

Miss Molly's Bed & Breakfast.

the market, numerous hotels, bathhouses, and saloons developed in the area. One such establishment opened in 1910, and was a rooming house arranged with nine rooms encircling a large, center parlor that could be rented by the day or week. By the 1920s, records show that a right "proper" lady, named Amelia Eimer, managed the place under the name, Palace Rooms. It was a successful business and continued through the prohibition years under different management and the name The Oasis.

By the 1940s, big meat packing companies such as Armour & Swift were attracted to the area by city incentives and brought with them workers needing to blow off a little steam and a weekly paycheck. Cowboys competing in the local rodeo circuit also wandered its streets, as well as servicemen looking for a good time before shipping off to war. It was in this environment that a wily entrepreneur named Miss Josie King made her appearance. She bought the boarding house, calling it the Gayette Hotel, and turned it into a proper sporting house. For a price, scantily clad girls were paraded out into the central parlor for a gentleman to make his selection, before the two would retire to one of the rooms for a night of passion.

There are many tales from this period, including one concerning a young man who fell in love with one of the working girls. So enamoured was he by her beauty that he vowed to make her his bride and constantly pestered her with proposals of marriage. Unable to stand his advances any longer, the girl simply packed up and moved

The Miss Josie's Room.

away without leaving a forwarding address. The young man was crushed by her departure, but Miss Josie took pity on him and told him that she had a girl so beautiful it would make him forget all about his lost love. With nothing to lose, the young man went to one of the rooms and knocked as he had been instructed to do. When the door swung open, there stood the spitting image of his dear old mother in her younger days. Shocked by the resemblance he fled that day never to return and later became a prominent religious leader.

As the cattle trade faded and the neighborhood changed again, the Gayette Hotel closed its doors and Miss Josie King was never be heard from again. For a time it became an art gallery, with the encircling rooms turned into artists' studios. Then in 1989, Mark and Susan Hancock bought the former bawdy house and restored it to its previous glory with artifacts from its earlier period; giving each room a unique western theme. It was at this time that the now refurbished bed and breakfast received the name Miss Molly's, after the term used for the lead cow in a cattle drive.

Today the stockyards have changed considerably and I doubt the cowboys that once sauntered down its streets would recognize it. Yet twice a day tourists can still glimpse cattle drives down the main thoroughfare for the amusement of crowds, although the herd is much smaller now. If you do stumble upon Miss Molly's and choose to walk up the steep metal staircase, the current owner, Tiffany Hicks, will be happy to show you around the place and tell you all about the ghosts that haunt it.

It's hard to say when the haunting truly began, but guests of Miss Molly's have reported the apparitions of several female ghosts about the old place. A local journalist reported one encounter during his stay in what's called the 'Cowboy Room' and is decorated in the fashion of an old bunkhouse, complete with twin iron beds and a potbellied stove. According to him, he was suddenly awakened from a deep sleep to find the figure of a young blonde at the foot of his bed gazing seductively at him. Before he could even raise himself up the figure vanished before his eyes.

Another account involves an Englishman staying alone in the 'Cattle Baron's' room, which is decorated in the plush style that a cattle baron might have been used to, with a large, carved oak bed below mounted longhorns. He too was awakened one night from his sleep to find a woman at the foot of his bed staring at him. Her figure cast in the light coming from the transom over the door. This time she was an elderly woman dressed in a sunbonnet and period clothing, and the owners think it might have been the protective spirit of Miss Amelia Eimer checking in on things.

The current owners are no strangers to the ghosts of their Bed and Breakfast and claim to have experienced cold spots, unusual perfumed fragrances, seen objects move by themselves, and had guests report being touch by an unseen presence. Even employees find themselves affected and one former owner of the establishment claims that a housekeeper was once scared off the job. When asked what the trouble was she reported that she kept finding coins in rooms where there had been no guests. When she removed the coins and finished cleaning, she returned to find them once again where she had removed them.

The ghostly gals of Miss Molly's never seem intent on harming anyone and the owners feel they're more protective than anything else. While talking to the owners I couldn't help but feel that maybe they were watching me as well. So if you've a mind to stay the night and see for yourself whether or not the spirits will make an appearance, go ahead. Even if they don't show, the beauty of the place and the excellent service will bring you back again.

Miss Molly's Bed & Breakfast, 109 West Exchange Avenue, Fort Worth, Texas 76106 Web: www.missmollyshotel.com

The Spirits that Never Checked Out

"Ghosts seem harder to please than we are;
it is as though they haunted for haunting sake–
much as we relive, brood, and smolder over our pasts."
- Elizabeth Bowen,
preface to *The Second Ghost* book

Just a stone's throw down the street from Miss Molly's Bed and Breakfast sits the Stockyard's Hotel, another popular Fort Worth destination and one that I came to find had a long history of unusual activity. Both guests and employees at this fine establishment have for years reported the presence of apparitions in its hallways and staircases at night. Since the two locations were so close to one another I just couldn't pass on the opportunity of paying a visit to the Stockyard's grand old lady and perhaps meeting these unearthly guests who wouldn't check out.

Erected on the corner of Exchange and Main streets in 1907 by Colonel Thomas M. Thannisch, the hotel was the crown jewel of the city in a time when the cattle industry was in full swing. Its elegant furnishings and fine displays drew everyone from traveling cowboys to foreign dignitaries and, as a testament to its luxury, each of its three floors boasted its very own bathroom. Make no doubt about it though, despite the hotel's grandeur the stockyards was still the ruff and tumble place of gaming parlors and saloons.

Entrance to the Stockyard's Hotel.

Gunfights were known to erupt right outside its doors as cowboys settled their disputes in the street. In one of Fort Worth's more famous shootouts, the legendary "Longhaired Jim" Courtright met his end just outside the hotel after calling the owner of the White Elephant Saloon, Luke Short, out for a showdown. Courtright was good with a gun, maybe even the best in town depending on whom you asked, but Short got the drop on him nonetheless and filled him with enough lead to send him to his maker.

In the one hundred years since the hotel was constructed it has changed names from the Chandler Hotel, to the Plaza Hotel, and finally the Stockyard's Hotel. In 1984, it was given a face-lift by then-owners Tom Yater and Marshall Young, who expanded the interior to its present 52-room layout. Not to worry though, for those of you thinking about spending the night, each room has its own bathroom now.

As I entered the Stockyard's Hotel's spacious lobby with its over-stuffed, leather furniture and western art, I could see why it has attracted so many famous personalities over the years. Some of the guests to have graced its rooms include Willie Nelson, George Straight, Garth Brooks, and some of the richest cattle and cotton kings this side of the Rio Grande. The two former guests that attracted my attention the most however were none other than the ill-famed bank robbers Bonnie Parker and Clyde Barrow.

In 1932, as the two were shooting their way across the southwest, they stopped at the Stockyard's Hotel to lay low for a spell. The story goes that the two bandits were actually casing a bank directly across the street from their room when authorities got wind of their plans and foiled the plot. Others tell that they did manage to pull off the bank job and left town with an undisclosed sum of money. Either way, fate would eventually deal the two a bum hand. One year later, on May 23, 1934, the two young lovers were gunned down on a dirt road in Louisiana by a posse of law enforcement officials; ending their bloody career.

Although the hotel's management doesn't believe that the two criminals are responsible for the building's haunting, they were generous enough to show me the actual room they stayed in. The 'Bonnie and Clyde Suite', as it's called (room 305), features a king size bed and its very own gaming table if your in the mood for a little Texas Hold'em. Historical artifacts line the walls including photographs of the two lovers and newspaper clippings of their exploits. My personal favorites however were Bonnie's .38 revolver and a poem she wrote to Clyde.

Bonnie and Clyde may not haunt the hotel, but management and staff here believes that another phantom wanders its halls at night. Affectionately known as Jesse, this spirit appears attired as a cowboy, complete with boots and spurs. During his brief appearances it's reported that he seems entirely oblivious to those around him as if unaware of their presence. At other times the spirit only manifests as the sound of booted footsteps echoing down the corridors, accompanied by the jingling of his spurs. Why he haunts the place is a bit of a mystery, but many think he may have come out on the losing end of a gunfight outside the hotel in its rowdier days.

Staircase where the phantom cowboy has been seen.

Another earthbound spirit unwilling to leave the place is thought to be a former employee named Jake. After twenty years of dedicated service to the hotel as a houseman delivering messages to the guest's rooms, Jake finally passed on. Soon however, strange incidents began occurring around the hotel, convincing the staff that Jake had returned again to resume his earthly duties. The lobby's elevators are known to move between floors unoccupied. When repairmen have been called out to service them, they were at a lost to explain the odd mechanical behavior. What some employees find truly disturbing, though, are the unusual late night calls that come into the front desk from a nonexistent extension that cannot be transferred or put on hold.

To be sure, the Stockyard's Hotel has seen its share of history, but even if you're not a ghost enthusiast then its plush surroundings and fine dining are worth the visit. As I wandered a bit, admiring the feel of the place and the art that decorates it, I listened very carefully for the sound of spurs across the floorboards. I even went as far as to linger in front of the elevator, hoping it would open for me by itself. It didn't. If, however, you do decide to pay the hotel a visit, the accommodating staff is always ready to entertain their guests with stories of the ghosts said to still haunt the place. Who knows? If you stay the night there, you just might run into one of those ghosts yourself. Either way it's worth the stay.

The Stockyard's Hotel, 109 East Exchange Avenue, Fort Worth, Texas 76106
Web: www.stockyardshotel.com

The House that Swift Built

*"Man is a mere phantom as he goes to and fro:
He bustles about, but only in vain; he heaps up
wealth, not knowing who will get it."*
                                        - Psalms 39:6

At the eastern edge of the stockyards, just beyond the well-lit gift shops and steakhouses that claim the area, you will find a low hill over-looking the cattle pens that once made the city famous. Atop the hill sits a structure that has for years attracted the interests of writers and ghost hunters alike with tales of shadowy figures lurking inside its dark rooms. In addition, it's said that a phantom can be seen at night staring out from the top windows at those who venture too far from the noise and lights of the tourist attractions.

Located at 600 East Exchange Avenue, the former Swift Meat Packing offices is all that remains of a once massive complex of warehouses, meat processing plants, and auction houses. When I pulled up one late and misty evening to walk the grounds and peer in through its windows the atmosphere itself seemed to lend a rather spooky element. I knew I was looking at the last of a once proud cattle empire that had breathed life into this city helping to make it what it is today.

In 1893, Greenlief W. Simpson, a wealthy Bostonian,

Swift Meatpacking Offices.

moved to the city and purchased the Fort Worth Union Stockyards. Simpson was a man who understood money and better yet, how to make it. He began by offering ranchers fifty cents more per head of cattle than rival Midwest markets such as Kansas City and Chicago. Soon cattle began pouring into the city, infusing it with a much-needed new life. In order to sustain the heavy purchases and ensure the success of his enterprise, Simpson knew he needed a company to process and ship the meat throughout the country. Therefore, he and other city businessmen offered large subsidies and partial ownership in the stockyards to both Swift and Armour, in an enticement to relocate to Fort Worth.

The bid worked and in the late 1890s, the era's two largest meatpackers accepted the proposal with Swift opening its doors in 1904. Things took off quickly from there and within six months both companies spent nearly six million dollars purchasing cattle, hogs, and sheep. Livestock once bound for slaughterhouses and rail stops in the Midwest now made its way to Fort Worth for processing. This early success led Swift to expand its operations, adding a canning factory and increasing the size of the holding pens to accommodate even more livestock. By 1958, the Swift facility in Fort Worth was valued at 10 million dollars and employed as many as 2,000 workers.

Yet for all its initial expansion and profit, history often shows us that all things, even powerful cattle empires, eventually come to an end. As markets changed competitors proved too much and with advances in industry technologies, such as the refrigerated railcar, Fort Worth began to lose its importance. Ironically, it was Swift Company founder, Gustavus Franklin Swift, who invented the ice-cooled railcar that allowed meat to be dressed and shipped all over the world. Before this technological breakthrough, livestock had to be slaughtered and placed in barrels of salt for shipment. This process necessitated that markets be closed to their source. Now with greater shipping options an era of cheap beef ushered in, spelling doom for the industry's profit margin.

By the 1970s, efforts to save the plant were failing and soon after it was forced to close its doors for good. Later that decade two massive fires raged through the former plant destroying all but the administrative offices on their hilltop perch. It then sat dormant, collecting dust, until the 1970s, when it was purchased and turned into an Italian eatery called the Spaghetti Warehouse. Known for its hearty fare and unique combination of spices, the new business prospered until it too closed in 2003.

It was from its time as a restaurant that most of the paranormal activity was reported. Employees claimed that after closing each night weird noises could be heard in the empty, upper rooms—noises that sounded like shuffling footsteps moving about. Once, while locking up for the evening the night manager was just finishing up his paperwork when he heard a disturbance coming from the bar. It was 2:30 in the morning and the manager knew he was the only one left in the building. Fearing a possible intruder he investigated the sounds and encountered the dark, shadowy figure of a man sitting at the bar. When he approached the figure it turned slowly towards him and vanished before his very eyes.

During a similar incident, another night manager was closing up when he too received a good scare. He knew the stories being passed around by the staff about the ghost of a man who died in the former plant fire, but he paid little attention to them. To him they were nothing more than that—stories. He followed the usual lockup procedures of carefully checking the building, locking the doors, and setting the alarm. It wasn't until he left the building and began making his way to his car that he felt something was wrong. Turning his gaze back to the building he gasped as he noticed the figure of someone staring down at him from one of the upper windows. Too afraid to risk an encounter with someone or something in the dark building alone, he jumped into his car and sped away. The next day when he opened the restaurant for business the building was empty, with no sign of forced entry, and the security alarm was still set.

Today, what remains of the old Swift building is being gutted for corporate office space and is closed to the public. While walking its grounds I did happen into the night security guard, who confided in me that strange things still happen here at night. More than once, he recounted, while patrolling the interior alone he felt something watching him. He smiled when I told him that I was writing about the place and even allowed me to take a few photographs before politely shooing me off.

After thanking him, I made my way back through the cold mist to the streetlights of the parking lot at the base of the hill. I did look back once or twice to see if anyone was watching me from the building's dark interior, but to my disappointment the windows were empty. Who the shadowy watcher of the old Swift building might be is unknown. Could it be a victim of the massive plant fire, earthbound to haunt the place where he or she died? Maybe it's old Gustavus Swift himself looking out that window at night, wondering where his empire went.

Former Swift Meat Packing Office, 600 East Exchange Avenue, Fort Worth, Texas 76106

The Scent of Flowers

"I am thinking of the lilac-trees,
That shook their purple plumes,
And when the sash was open,
Shed fragrance through the room."
- Anna S. Stephens,
The Old Apple Tree

For those wishing to capture a glimpse of what early life was like for Fort Worth's hardy pioneers, there's no better place than the Log Cabin Village. For the price of admission, just a few bucks, you can travel back in time and stroll through park-like grounds dotted with authentic log cabins lovingly restored and furnished with authentic artifacts from the era. Throughout the village you'll also find an assorted cast of historical re-enactors twisting wool into thread, beating hot metal into horseshoes, and telling stories of life on the western frontier. If you're lucky enough, or unlucky, depending on your view, you might just run into a good deal more and see the park's resident ghost. Not to worry if you don't see her though, because if you keep your nose sharp, you can smell the fragrance of her passing.

The Log Cabin Village can be found near the banks of the Trinity River just south of the city's downtown area at 2100 Log Cabin Village Lane. It began in 1950 when the president of the Texas State Historical Association, Fred Cotton, in conjunction with W. A. Schmid Jr. of the Pioneer Texas Heritage Committee, lobbied the City of Fort Worth to preserve the few examples of early pioneer life still remaining. Several log cabins scattered about the countryside of Parker, Tarrant, and Milam counties were chosen for the project. Board by board they were taken apart, numbered, and moved to the museum complex where they were reassembled to depict a village from the 1800s.

Betty Regester was chosen as historical curator to get the museum off the ground and lost no time in researching the individual cabins, organizing volunteers, and collecting donations. After a heroic effort on her part, the Log Cabin Village officially opened to the public in 1966 as a living museum where anyone with an appreciation of the past could watch life from the period unfold right before their very eyes.

It wasn't until the Foster cabin was installed in the park that visitors and staff started reporting encounters with the apparition that may have come with it. The Foster cabin once rested on the banks of the Brazos River near the cotton-producing town of Port Sullivan in Milam County. Using slave labor, huge, hand-hewed oak and cedar timbers were collected from the river bottoms and used to construct the home sometime between 1850-54. The original owner, Harry Foster, was pleased with the impressive two-story cabin that sat facing the rich fields of cotton and named the place Lucky Ridge. If you try to find the community of Port Sullivan on a map today, you

The Foster Cabin.

won't be able to. The local economy relied heavily on the cotton enterprise and slave labor for its industry. In the aftermath of the American Civil War the area was decimated, leaving behind only a few weathered tombstones in an overgrown cemetery to mark its passing.

The Foster clan moved to the area from Mississippi shortly after the new Republic of Texas gained its independence from Mexico in 1836. This included Harry Foster, his wife Martha, who died in the cabin in the 1870s, several daughters and two sons, William Henry and Joseph Ancell. By the 1880s, census records showed two new additions to the household, a Mrs. Jane Holt and her six-year-old son. It's speculated that Jane was acting as a housekeeper to the family after the death of Mrs. Foster and served as a nurse to one of the boys who lost an arm fighting in the Civil War. This wasn't an uncommon arrangement at the time and Jane herself is thought to have been the widow of a local physician. One of the employees I spoke with about Jane thought that the two might also have fallen in love and married, although there is no actual proof of their union. What we do know is that when the next population census rolled around ten years later, it did not list a Mrs. Jane Holt as part of the household and it's believed that she died during this period.

The cabin remained in the Foster family until the early 1900s, when it was rented to poor tenant farmers trying to scratch a living from the soil. Eventually, when the cabin fell into disrepair and became uninhabitable, it was abandoned in 1939. The years came and went taking their toll on the vacant structure and it would have certainly moldered away to nothing if it hadn't been donated to the park in 1969.

The staff that works in the Foster cabin, which also serves as the village's general store and visitor center, now think that it's haunted by one or even both of the women who once lived and died there. Several visitors to the cabin have reported the apparition of an attractive female in her 30s or 40s in the upstairs bedroom. She's said to be dressed in a long, black skirt and purple shirt with the leg O mutton type sleeves commonly worn by women during that period. Usually when she appears the smell of lilacs fill the air and the room takes on a heavy, oppressive feeling. Others report that when the ghost is around the temperature drops dramatically and an electrical sensation causes the hair on their arms and neck to stand on end. On one occasion while the village was closed, museum manager Kelli Pickard and educator Rena Lawrence were working in the Foster cabin. They heard the doorbell to the cabin ring, followed by the opening of the front door and footsteps down the short hallway to their office. Surprised to hear a guest enter they hurried out into the hallway to find no one there.

On August 19, 1987, three documentary filmmakers set out to discover for themselves if the legends of a ghostly presence in the Foster cabin were true. As one of the men involved in the project, Terry Smith, made his way through the cabin alone he started to hear the sound of footsteps approaching him. It was a noticeable sound he would describe, like someone wearing old-fashioned Victorian style lady's shoes. The steps came right up to him as he felt the floorboards under his feet lower slightly from their weight. Later he replayed a tape recorder he was running at the time and discovered that it had captured the ghostly footsteps on tape.

After the apparition gave several visitors a good scare, the museum closed the room to the public and converted it into office space for the village staff. With the upper level of the cabin off limits it didn't give me much of a chance to poke around. I did wonder about the fragrance of lilacs that seems to manifest whenever the spirit shows up. Could it be that the ghost of Jane or Martha simply likes the smell of lilacs? I would later learn that early settlers often planted lilacs around their cabins, much as we do today with our modern flower gardens. It also made me wonder about the deaths of the two women that took place in the cabin. Perhaps as one of them lay dying in her bed the last sensation they experienced was the sweet fragrance of lilacs coming in through the window before they closed their eyes forever.

The Log Cabin Village, 2100 Log Cabin Village Lane, Fort Worth, Texas 76109 Web: www.logcabinvillage.org

---

The Guardian Spirit of Peter Brothers Hats

*"We've been here since 1911 and
we're not going anywhere."*
- Tom Peters,
founder of Peter Brothers Hats

The Peter Brothers Hat Company is a business that has seen its share of change over the years. If you ask owner Joe Peters the secret of his success, he'll tell you it may be in part due to a watchful family spirit. Situated just off of Sundance Square, the business has been in the Peters family for close to one hundred years. It began with two Greek brothers, Tom and Jim Peters, who changed their family name when they reached Ellis Island. Fueled with the great American dream of prosperity and success the two immigrants made their way to Fort Worth and opened their own shoeshine parlor. Through hard work and perseverance the new business grew, eventually employing as many as 36 shine men. When fashions changed so too did the resilient Peters brothers, converting their shine parlor into a hat shop in 1911. The hat trade was something the brothers knew well and not only had Tom dyed hats in Greece, but he had also worked for John Stetson in Pennsylvania for a time.

When Jim passed away in 1933, the insurance money allowed the ever growing Peters family to purchase the

Peter Brothers Hats Co.

building for the sum of $15,000. During World War II the top floor of the building was turned into a hat factory for the U.S. military, which operated until the end of the Korean War. To this day the family business continues in its fine tradition under the ownership of father and son Joe Sr. and Joe Jr., where you can find everything from hand-made Western Stetsons to Indiana Jones style fedoras.

Even though Tom Peters passed away in June of 1991, at over 100-years-old, the Peters family has

51

come to feel that his spirit returns to watch over the place. Objects often move around by themselves or in some cases disappear altogether. On other occasions, Joe Sr. claims that hats safely secured on long display hooks, are mysteriously knocked to the ground. This, he believes, is his father's way of telling him that he's still around to make sure the business runs as it should.

There are some however, that will tell you that Tom Peters isn't the only spirit checking up on the place. When the business expanded into Eli's Pizza shop next door they might have inherited another spirit as well. In March of 1991, the owner of Eli's Pizza Shop, Gary Wiese, told *Fort Worth Star-Telegram* reporter Mary Roger about other odd occurrences in the building he attributed to a former employee of his. Jack Martin was a dishwasher and odd job man for about ten years before he died. Soon after his funeral, at 4:15 p.m. everyday the door to the pizza shop would open and close by itself, as if some invisible presence were entering. Oddly enough this happened to correspond to the time when Jack would have normally left for the day. Jack's spirit also seemed to have a rather playful side and loved to torment new employees. Whenever someone new was hired and walked past Jack's old dishwasher it sprang to life, soaking them with water. This shocked many of the workers because the machine had safety features designed to prohibit this from happening. For it to run, the doors had to be closed and the start button held down for several seconds.

In a final twist, employees have heard the sounds of low moaning floating up the dark basement stairs. Some claim that the eerie sounds are connected to the death of a former employee who stumbled down the steps to his death in the days when it was still a shoeshine parlor. So whether you walk through the doors of the Peter Brothers Hat Company looking for a fine quality hat or a good ghost story, the employees will be happy to assist you in trying on either.

Peter Brothers Hat Company, 909 Houston Street, Fort Worth, Texas 76102
Web: www.peterbros.com

Hats that are mysteriously knocked off their racks.

Dining with a Ghost

"...chasing ghost stories in restaurants
is a dangerous thing for me."
- Mitchel Whitington,
Ghosts of North Texas

As I mentioned earlier in the book, the "Hell's Half Acre" section of Fort Worth has enjoyed a rather odious reputation. Usually shortened to the "Acre," the term first appeared in local newspapers to describe a lower end of town filled with saloons, dancehalls, and gambling joints intermixed with more legitimate businesses. The "Acre" was where a cowboy went if he were either looking for a little excitement or a whole lot of trouble. As the city grew so to did the "Acre," covering an area as large as four city blocks, which amounted to, despite its name, much more than a mere half acre. In 1876, when the city was divided into political jurisdictions the quarter comprising the "Acre" was also known as the "Bloody Third Ward."

The more law-abiding citizens of Fort Worth had always looked upon the "Acre" as a constant source of concern. Law enforcement statistics show that as much as fifty percent of the violent crimes committed in the city originated in the "Acre" and on any given Saturday night as many as thirty people were hauled off to jail.

Over time this began to hit the city where it hurt the most—in the pocket book. Businesses began suffering as out-of-towners fell prey to the card sharks, con men, and pickpockets that roamed the streets. To add insult to injury the city became extremely embarrassed when it became public that stagecoach robbers were using the area as a hideout for their criminal operations.

There were two incidents in 1889 that placed pressure on city leaders to begin curtailing some of the worst establishments. The first was the famous shootout that cost "Longhaired Jim" Courtright his life. Although the gunfight didn't take place in the "Acre" per se, it did focus attention on the city's shady underworld. The second involved the gruesome murder of a prostitute named Sally, who was found nailed to the door of a building. These blatant acts of disregard for the law outraged the city's populous and began a grassroots movement by church leaders to clean up the city streets.

In 1911, Reverend J. Frank Norris launched just such a campaign from his pulpit at the First Baptist Church. His attacks were not only aimed at the vices of the "Acre," but at what he came to see as a corrupt and complacent city leadership. Whether or not he fully understood the weight his preaching would carry is uncertain, but it did not go unnoticed by his opponents. In retaliation for Rev. Norris's attacks, the First Baptist Church was burned to the ground on February 14, 1912, and to drive the point home a bundle of burning rags was thrown onto his porch in an attempt to burn the parsonage. One month later the arsonists returned again, this time succeeding in burning down the house. A sensational trial resulted with threats and accusations flying back and fourth on both sides. At one point, the Rev. Norris was even brought to trial on accusations that he burned his own church down in order to garner sympathy for his cause. By 1917, the embattled Reverend, along with a new city administration, convinced the federal government to declare martial law in the "Acre." Now with troops on the streets and stiff jail sentences awaiting offenders, "Hell's Half Acre" was finally tamed.

Walking through its streets today you would never guess at its lawless past. Urban growth and rising property values have changed the dusty roads and two-story saloons into glittering high rises and traffic congested streets. One of the few remaining buildings to have survived the ravages of progress was once a popular bathhouse. Cowboys worn thin on the trail could get a hot bath and a shave before venturing onto the streets for a round of cards or perhaps the company of a professional lady for the evening. Legend has it that one day, just such a gentleman lay soaking in a hot tub when an unseen gunman came up from behind and shot him through the head. The gunman was never identified nor was the motivation for the killing ever clear. The shooting could very well have been the result of some previous exchange of words, or money owed, or even, as was all to often the case, simply being in the wrong place at the wrong time. Even if we lack the true modus operandi we do know that many believe the spirit of the murder victim haunts the building to this day.

Entrance to Del Frisco's Double Eagle Steakhouse.

Situated within walking distance of Sundance Square and the convention center, the old bathhouse is now Del Frisco's Double Eagle Steakhouse. For those of you (like me) who love a good ghost story as much as a juicy steak, Del Frisco's is where you can find both. Just walking into the spacious two-story building with its dark wood paneling and succulent aromas, you know you're in for a culinary experience. The chef told me that the meat is so fresh it's driven in twice a day in un-re-frigerated cars and cut straight from the loin when the ticket enters the kitchen. Known for their prime aged, corn fed beef and cold-water Australian lobster tails, it was hard not to forget why I was here. Ghost hunting after all can be hard work and, as I pushed back my empty plate with a deep sigh of bliss, I managed to get a few of the employees to tell me about the ghost that haunts the place.

Despite the good food and friendly atmosphere many employees have experienced an invisible presence that follows them throughout different parts of the building. Often at night while wiping off tables or counting well-de-served tips, they report hearing footsteps on the staircase or in the closed off rooms of the upper level. Chilling cold spots can be felt at different times, along with the sen-sation that something unnatural is watching them from the darker corners of the room. One server recounted that while clearing tables on the second floor one night, the temperature in the room suddenly dropped and an invisible presence grabbed both of her shoulders from behind. The staff here assures me though, that although the ghost has been around for as long as anyone can remember, its actions are never threatening. According to them the ghost is just part of the place.

In all of my research, one of the questions I try to ask myself is, why a spirit seems bent on remaining earthbound? It's a difficult question to say the least and one whose answer varies from spirit to spirit. But could the unnatural death of the gentleman as he soaked in his tub have left his spirit confused, unable to comprehend it no longer existed in the flesh, or is it something more sinister? Is the invisible spirit of Del Frisco's wandering through the place still looking to seek revenge on the man that killed him? More unanswered questions. I knew why I was still here, however, and, after finishing off my Banana's Foster, I couldn't help but imagine that if I was a ghost, what better place to be. Be forewarned however, if you come here for the ghost, you'll stay for the food and if you leave an empty place at your table you just might be dining with a ghost.

Del Frisco's Double Eagle Steakhouse,
812 Main Street, Fort Worth, Texas 76102
Web: www.delfriscos.com

The Spirits Upstairs

"People live upstairs - but you'll never see them."
- a former Jett Building tenant

At the busy southwest corner of Third and Main streets sits a building that almost seems out of place surrounded by the modern offices and high rises threatening to engulf it. Just off festive Sundance Square, the Jett Building traces its long roots back to the outlaw days of the "Acre," when it acted as the headquarters for the Northern Texas Traction Company. The NTT, as it was known by its shorter name, provided the first inner city rail service running thirty-five miles from Fort Worth to Dallas. In the one hundred plus years that it has occupied this little corner of downtown, the Jett Building has transformed itself time and again as businesses came and went, each seemingly unable to make a stay of it for very long. Over time the Jett Building has appeared in numerous books and newspaper articles, not as much for its lengthy history, but for the ghostly inhabitants of its upper floors.

The mystery of the Jett Building begins with its very origin, which itself seems somewhat in dispute. A three-story, rectangular structure of brick masonry in the early modern style, it was said to model Frank Lloyd Wright's Larkin Building in Buffalo, New York. Research shows

Entrance to the Jett Building.

that it was constructed in 1902 as the NTT's main terminal and ticket station. Tax records from the era paint a different picture however, and don't begin to show the building's completion until 1920. Finally, there are some that claim that historical references demonstrate the structure existed as early as the 1880s.

What we do know is that after a hard fought battle with the automobile industry the NTT stopped service and closed its doors in 1934, as Americans turned to the ever more affordable automobile for transportation. A candy factory filled its shoes for a time and soon after, a title company. During the 1940s, it changed hands again to become a sandwich shop, and a series of ghastly murders took place on the empty third floor. It's said that two women were dragged or lured upstairs and then brutally dispatched by a serial killer. Whether or not this account actually took place is hard to tell because the story has become so intertwined with the legends surrounding the place. It's said though, usually rather dramatically, that the upstairs sinks are still stained with blood from the killer's attempts to dispose of the bodies.

The building sat vacant through much of the 1970s, as the city's downtown district faced an economic slump. The 1980s ushered in a new push to revitalize the downtown and attract more tourist dollars to the area. In 1985, the building was given a new lease on life when the city hired Richard Haas to design the "Chisholm Trail" mural façade that graces the south and west sides of the building, to commemorate the cattle drives of the 1800s. The revitalization of the Jett Building brought in new businesses, but once again they failed to find their place for long. Some of these included companies as diverse as Fort Worth's Books & Video, the Deep Ellum Café, Smokey Toes Island Grill, and Pangburn's Chocolates.

Regardless of which business occupied the building at the time, rumors continued to circulate that the place was haunted and some owners found workers hard to keep employed after encountering one of the ghosts. In 1983, while remodeling the moldy basement into space for a bookstore, one of the plumbers quit rather suddenly. When asked why he refused to finish the job, he claimed that while in the basement he witnessed the apparition of a woman floating down the staircase. Encounters with the phantom woman would be repeated numerous times throughout the years. On Halloween night in 1933, an unsuspecting bartender was closing the upstairs bar for the night when he happened to glance in a mirror and find the shadowy figure of a woman watching him. When he turned she was gone.

Unexplained noises are often heard coming from the usually unoccupied, third floor as well. Sounds of some-one walking in women's shoes or of someone dragging a heavy object across the floor have been reported. In one case, an employee stayed late to stock the shelves of the basement bookstore when he heard what sounded like a metal ball rolling in a roulette wheel, accompanied by the sounds of music. Knowing that he was alone and the building locked up tight, he called security officers

Jett Building Mural by Richard Haas.

to investigate. After searching every nook and cranny of the place they found nothing that could have produced the sounds. Others have heard the sounds as well, describing it as the sound of a child's ball rolling around the floors of the upper level.

Unlike some of the other haunted locations we've examined where the ghosts are accepted or even welcome as part of the place, the ghosts of the Jett Building have been known to get down right mean. Objects are repeatedly been broken or destroyed by the malicious ghosts. One night a former bar manager heard a terrible crashing sound from the third floor storage area. Racing up the old wooden staircase to the source of the commotion, she stopped in her tracks when she reached the landing. Right before her very eyes, wineglasses were falling from a rack and shattering one by one. The ghosts also seemed to have taken a disliking to the bookstore when it resided there and it was not uncommon for employees to open for the morning and find books shredded and tossed onto the floor. When asked, as a matter of curiosity, which books the spooky vandals chose, it was noted they were usually science fiction novels.

The range of their assaults has targeted more than just inanimate objects however, extending to some scary situations for people too. One former tenant spent a harrowing night locked in the building as a result of spiritual machinations. As he was closing up for the night he entered the basement to secure an office door. When he entered the room, more of a closet really, the heavy door slammed shut and locked from the outside leaving him trapped in the confined space. The next morning employees freed him and although he wasn't physically hurt he was visibly shaken by the experience.

Today, despite its many failures, the Jett Building is home to both a Jamba Juice and the western radio station, 95.9 FM "The Ranch." In an October 16, 2006 article of the *Fort Worth Star-Telegram*, radio employees were asked if they had run into their ghostly neighbors upstairs yet. Michael Margrave, the station engineer, claimed that he witnessed the dark form of a cowboy descending the stairs from the first floor to the basement.

"The third time I looked at it, I could see through it," he said in response.

For the most part however, the employees of "The Ranch" try and keep a live and let live attitude when it comes to their ghostly tenants. A large note on the basement storage room door sums up their philosophy perfectly, "We ain't afraid of no ghosts…but please leave the lights on."

The Jett Building, 400 Main Street,
Fort Worth, Texas 76102

Literary Spirits

"After a while you understand nothing is going to hurt you...that it's a friendly presence."
- Brian Perkins Sr.,
bookstore owner

As Brian Perkins, Sr. tells the story it wasn't some "dark and stormy night," but a beautiful Sunday morning much like any other. He was alone on the third floor of the bookstore dusting the old books and restocking the shelves when he heard an unusual sound. From somewhere among the twisting maze of bookracks someone was thumbing rapidly through the pages of book after book. Knowing the place was locked up tighter than Fort Knox, Brian set aside his dust rag in order to investigate the noise. Weaving through the maze of books, taking each turn with caution, he was just upon what he thought was the source of the sound when it stopped. To his astonishment the aisle he turned into was empty, save for a pile of discarded books on the floor that someone or something had thrown carelessly to the ground. An eerie sensation filled him, causing the hair to stand on his neck and arms as he stooped over to clean up the unexplained mess.

In the time since Brian Perkins Sr. purchased the old Barber's Bookstore from Irene Evans in 1969,

Barber's Bookstore.

he has seen many things he hadn't thought possible before. Mrs. Evans had parted with her beloved bookstore to care for her terminally ill husband without mentioning the place came complete with its own set of ghosts. A rather spunky lady to say the least, she later died at the age of fifty-three, in a sky-diving accident. Before Mrs. Evans, the three-story art décor style building at Eighth and Throckmorton streets, watched a number of owners come and go. First opened by Bert and Alice Barber in 1925, the business lays claim to being the oldest continually running bookstore in all of Texas.

The building however wasn't always home to the works of great writers such as Shakespeare and King, but was a brothel in the days of the "Acre" known as the Adams Hotel. Before the late Jules Goldstein passed away, he was fond of telling stories from his boyhood in the "Acre." The hotel he described was a busy place both night and day where cowboys could hire the services of a beautiful woman for a little company. The working girls would hang out of the second-story windows and announce to passersbys their particular services, even flaunting their wares. As Jules would say, it was also a good place for the kids to scrounge up soda money on a hot day. The working girls hated the kids hanging out in front of the building interrupting their trade and tossed down coins for them to "take a hike."

Today the old Barber's Bookstore is called the Back Door Book Shop and is something of a hidden treasure trove for serious book connoisseurs. Thousands of titles lay stacked on shelves, leaning in corners, and even filling up staircases in room after room. Many of the books are not what you would find on today's bestseller's list and run the gambit from Texas history to obscure theological texts. Despite what seems a maddening organization system that defies logic, Brian Perkins Sr. can tell you where to find any book in the store. Perhaps it only adds to the allure of the place, but a person could happily spend hours hunting through piles of books, moving from one prize to another. Brian believes this is also what has kept the old place afloat over the years as colossal giants such as Barnes and Nobles moved into the area. Some of these books are such rarities they date back to the 1500s and sell for hundreds of dollars.

The Back Door Book Shop may hold more than just a few literary jewels however, and many have experienced the ghosts that haunt the place. One Sunday morning in May of 1995, the owner's son, Wesley Perkins, was busy working in an office on the third floor when he heard footsteps approaching. Startled by the noise he looked up to find a man in blue jeans and a T-shirt walking down the hallway outside the office. Springing from his desk, Wesley grabbed his gun from the top drawer and pursued the mysterious figure. As he explored the building from top to bottom however he found no one and could not explain how anyone could have entered the locked building.

Even the owner's pet seems to have had a few run-ins with the resident ghosts. Before coming to the bookstore Brian's pet cat was your typical friendly, little ball of fur that enjoyed nothing more than a scratch behind the ear or a soft lap to nap in. After settling into the new place its personality seemed to take a strange turn. It began acting jumpy and instead of exploring its new home it refused to enter the third floor altogether. There were even times when it hunched its back and hissed at the empty air as if it contained some invisible threat.

Much of the paranormal activity occurring in the bookstore seems to center on an interior staircase that was once part of the main entrance when the building housed the Adams Hotel. During its days as a brothel, a murder took place on the staircase that may shed some light on the identities of the spirits haunting the place. The story goes that one of the beautiful, young, working girls fell in love with a cowboy that frequented her bed and planned to run off and marry him. When the father of the girl found out she was working at the hotel and that she planned to elope with a no good traveling cowboy he became infuriated. Grabbing his gun he stormed off to bring his daughter home. As luck would have it, he arrived just as the cowboy was leaving his daughter's room and promptly gunned the young man down in the stairwell. We hear little of what happened to the father for committing the murder, but it is said that in a fit of grief the daughter soon after took her own life in room number 11.

Stairwell where phantom footsteps have been heard.

Now footsteps are reported on the staircase and shadowlike figures have been spotted climbing its steps before disappearing at the top. When the third floor was rented out to antique merchant years ago, room number 11 was constantly plagued by unusual activity. Workers opening up each morning often found the contents of the room in complete disarray. Many times items such as cups and saucers placed on shelves in the room flew off and crashed to the ground. During these manifestations a powerful, musty smell filled the room and more than one browsing customer left in a hurry after being touched by an unseen presence.

Jana Huges, who owns the Downtown Market and Deli that shares part of the building with the bookstore, believes that some of the ghostly activity may have spilled over into her business as well. Icy cold spots are sometimes felt in odd places about the deli and whenever she goes to the third floor alone she gets a creepy feeling like she's being watched. Much like the bookstore, when opening in the morning she sometimes finds items taken from the shelves and placed in the aisle floor. She doesn't really seem to mind the ghosts however, in fact when speaking to her you get the impression that she's rather proud the place is haunted and she's more than happy to share her stories.

"They don't eat much," she'll tell you. "I only regret that they don't clean up after themselves."

Whether the returning spirits are the ghosts of two star-crossed lovers who died in the building or some obsessed book lover still looking for a good deal, there is something strange going on at the Back Door Book Shop. Although the third floor is closed to anyone without an appointment, owner Brian Perkins, Sr. is happy to show guests around. He is after all these years convinced that the spirits who reside here are indeed friendly—well mostly friendly that is.

Back Door Book Shop, 901 South Throck-morton Street, Fort Worth, Texas 76102

Don't Let the Bed Ghost Bite

"Never walk near the bed; to a ghost your ankle
is your most vulnerable part - once in bed,
you're safe; he may lie around under the bed
all night, but you're safe as daylight. If you still
have doubts pull the blanket over your head."
- F. Scott Fitzgerald, *This Side of Paradise*

I remember as a child that one of the first ghosts I ever encountered happened to live under my very own bed. A foul, loathsome creature it was, who waited each night for the opportunity to snatch at any wayward foot or hand unfortunate enough to slip over the side. What it did with you once it dragged you under the bed was anyone's guess, but the thought was enough to make a young child shiver in fright. You were safe of course, while your parents were there tucking you in and the bedroom light remained on. Yet at some point, after the bedtime stories and prayers, the parents inevitably left the room and always flicked off the light when they went out. I managed to survive those years intact, despite the obvious danger of being eaten alive, but I learned several things during that time. The first is that under-the-bed ghosts really seem to get around and just about every child has one at some point or another. The second is that the worst torture in the world doesn't compare with

Texas White House Bed & Breakfast.

having to use the bathroom at 1 a.m. when a man-eating ghost lives under your bed. Finally, if you think the ghost under my bed was a nasty one, you should have seen the four-headed monster that lived in my closet.

My next stop was the Texas White House Bed and Breakfast—a place reputed to have a ghost haunting one of its rooms. The difference was that this one in particular wasn't satisfied with staying under the bed, but in some cases was known to climb right in with you. Located on Eighth Avenue, the bed and breakfast is just minutes away from such local attractions as the Kimball Art Museum, the Bass Performance Hall, and the Fort Worth Zoo. Whether it's a romantic getaway for two or a simple business trip, owners Grover McMains and his wife Jaime aspire to the philosophy that a little creativity goes a long way.

Initially built in 1910 by a Mr. Bishop for his son, the rambling country-style home with its expansive porch was instead sold to William B. Newkirk, who settled there with his new family. Life was good for William and his wife in their new home where the two worked hard to raise their four boys properly. William made his living in the investment business and could afford such a large house in one of Fort Worth's most affluent neighborhoods. Indeed fortune seemed to smile brightly on the Newkirk family until the stock market crashed in 1929. The economic hardships that followed were troubling and more so given the nature of Mr. Newkirk's business affairs. Yet like many American families that suffered through the Great Depression, the Newkirks pulled together and managed to survive. All four boys quit their studies and took jobs to help support the family, a true testament to the perseverance of a family in the midst of hardship.

As the nation fought its way out of the economic morass all four boys went on to serve in World War II. Remarkably all four Newkirks returned alive and each went on to start families of their own, with two of them leaving the area altogether. One of the remaining siblings, Richard Newkirk, even served as mayor of Fort Worth for a time. Yet no matter how far away they lived or how busy they became they still regarded the house on Eighth Avenue as their home. It remained a gathering place for the now extended family until Mrs. Newkirk's death in the home in 1967. William Newkirk died in the home a few years earlier and with the place now empty the surviving family members opted to sell the property.

Over the next twenty years or so it went on to house a number of small businesses including a restaurant from which the current Bed and Breakfast took its name. In 1994, the McMains took one look at the place and right away saw its potential. After two years of renovations the house finally saw life again, this time as a Bed and Breakfast. Three guestrooms occupy the main house, complete with king size beds and ornate bathrooms. The carriage house has been converted into suites fit for a king as well, with their own private whirlpools and saunas.

Admittedly the McMains may have gotten something else when they bought the house; something they hadn't bargained for. Since its opening in 1996, guests have periodically come down to breakfast and claimed that during the night an invisible presence tried to crawl into bed with them. Such tales would be easy to pass off as a dream or perhaps a case of bad digestion if they didn't all follow a particular pattern. All of the ghostly manifestations seem to center on the Lone Star Room. Decorated in antique mahogany furniture and claw-footed tub, this room was once the master bedroom of William Newkirk and his wife. An equally important factor in the haunting seems to do with the who—not the where. The ghost of the Texas White House only appears when there is a woman staying alone in the room. It has never appeared to a man, even if he were part of a couple.

One of the first stories repeated by a guest after a fitful night in the room centered on many of these details. The woman claimed that after preparing for bed she happily let her head hit the pillow when she felt someone lie down next to her. Rolling over in fright she discovered the huge bed was empty of all but her. Still, the uncanny sensation that someone was in the bed with her continued for several minutes, at which time she felt the presence slip off the bed and leave the room.

In an incident similar to the first, two women were staying in the very same room. They too were bedded down for the night, each positioned so that their backs were to one another. As they began drifting off to sleep, they sensed someone lying down between them. Perplexed by the sensation, one of the women reached over

The haunted Lone Star Room.

to turn on the light. Immediately the presence moved off the bed and out of the room. Just as the lamplight flooded the room however, a cell phone left on the night-stand started ringing, flashing, and vibrating as if all its functions had been activated at once. Checking the phone the women noted no incoming calls were listed and they were unable to explain the malfunction.

Cell phones are not the only electronic devices to act strangely when the ghost is present. One guest stated that she was lying in bed talking to her husband on the phone when the ceiling fan above began rotating. She found it disturbing at the time given the fact that there was no breeze in the room and the fan's switch was set in the off position. As soon as she made a comment to her husband over the phone about the oddity, the fan's motion abruptly stopped.

Of those that have encountered the invisible spirit of the Lone Star Room, each has claimed that it was unmistakably a strong, male presence that they felt. Although several of the women were given a good scare, none believed that the spirit had intended them any harm. Many surmise that the ghost haunting the Texas White House belongs to William Newkirk, who died there... possibly in the very same room. Perhaps it is William returning on nights to what he remembers as a happy home and climbing into what he still thinks is his bed. Regardless, that is, of the fact that there's someone already in it. Others have another explanation for the haunting. You see Mr. Newkirk is still a gentleman of his period and may feel the need to be protective when he finds a woman alone; and they say chivalry is dead.

I thought about staying the night in the haunted room, but since our ghost only appears to damsels in distress it seemed a bit pointless. Anyway, I think I had enough sleepless nights as a child to last a lifetime. I must say though, I think I would much rather have them lurking about under the bed, than in the covers with me.

The Texas White House, 1417 Eighth Avenue, Fort Worth, Texas 76104
www.texaswhitehouse.com

The "Castle of Cowtown"

"The ghosts you chase you never catch."
- John Malkovich

Once upon a time there was a beautiful princess that lived in a magic castle on a hill. That's the way fairy tales usually begin anyway, and then some knight comes ridding onto the scene trying to poke a dragon with a long sharp stick. Fort Worth has something of a fairy tale castle of its own as well; only the stories surrounding this one are a little bit different. Instead of a damsel in distress, this one involves a rich, young socialite who may have stuck around long after her party days on this earth ended. Granted this one doesn't have any jousting knights or fire-breathing dragons either, but it does have a team of ghost hunters that spent the night wandering through its darkened corridors in search paranormal activity. Now on with our story...

The "Castle of Cowtown" is more commonly known by its proper name, Thistle Hill. Originally the three-story Georgian mansion sat alone on a hill in the "Silk Stocking District" surrounded by rows of mansion-lined streets. Unfortunately time and progress have not been kind to the neighborhood and many of the stately homes that filled the area have fallen prey to the wrecking ball. Although Thistle Hill survived the destruction, it still seems pressed on every side by the paved streets and medical offices that

84

Thistle Hill Mansion.

have inched their way up to its very doors. Yet even today, just by looking at the place you can see that it was once meant as an expression of the wealth, pride, and ambition of its former owners. With over 11,000 square feet sectioned into eighteen rooms and six baths, the structure is composed of thick, brick walls and massive limestone pillars. Through the leaded-glass doors that mark the entrance you'll find an enormous, wooden staircase and an interior that looks like it could have been featured in *Life Styles of the Rich and Famous*. Many of the rooms are paneled in expensive, English Oak and cluttered with an array of paintings, period furniture, and statuary. What remains of the once expansive grounds are well manicured and festooned with flowers. Two other structures occupying the estate include a carriage house and an ornate water tower. The tower in question is what often gives the place its castle-like appearance and looks as if it were built to withstand a medieval siege. This led to the mansion appearing on an episode of *America's Castles* for the A&E Network.

Thistle Hill was built in 1904 by the legendary cattle Baron William T. Waggoner as a wedding gift for his daughter, Electra and son-in-law A.B. Wharton. He was initially worried the two would move to Philadelphia, Pennsylvania after their marriage and so wanted to entice them to stay. Waggoner was the stuff of Texas legends; a man who pulled himself up by his boot straps, so to speak, from a simple cattle driver to one of the most powerful men in the state. At his peak he held immense cattle, grazing ranges north and west of the city that were so large they spread over six counties. Cattle Barons like Waggoner were said to have ruled over more territory than most European nobility. The only difference being that the vast majority of their subjects were cattle not serfs.

Waggoner spared no expense when planning the wedding gift and hired Fort Worth's leading architectural firm, Sanguinet and Staats, who were responsible for some of the city's most famous buildings. The house, which sat in Fort Worth's most prestigious neighborhood, was eventually finished for the huge sum of $38,000. Electra and her husband moved into their new place after an extended honeymoon in Europe, living there until 1910. Before they placed it up for sale and moved to their ranch in Mt. Vernon, however, Electra gained quite the reputation as a socialite. She threw extravagant parties and balls that were often covered in the society section of the city's newspapers. These sometimes comprised hundreds of guests, that counted as the who's who of the American elite, including politicians, socialites, and early movie idols.

In 1911, a real estate tycoon named Winfield Scott bought Thistle Hill for $90,000 and began renovations amounting to an additional $100,000. It was meant to be the home he would raise his family in, but sadly Mr. Scott died before the house was completed. Instead, his wife Elizabeth Simmons Scott and their young son Winfield Scott, Jr. were left to occupy the home alone. The widow Mrs. Scott was nothing like her predecessor Electra Waggoner and was known more for her reserved and stately manner. Upon her death in 1938, Winfield Jr., always something of a black sheep in the family, quickly ran through his inheritance. In order to maintain his expensive lifestyle he auctioned off most of his mother's belongings and was forced to finally sell Thistle Hill when there was nothing left to pawn.

The property was soon picked up by the Girls Service League of Fort Worth for $17,500 and used as a dormitory for underprivileged girls looking to get back on their feet. They remained in the house until 1968 when they moved to another location, leaving the grand house to deteriorate. For a time it seemed the old place would go the way of all the other homes in the neighborhood, if it hadn't been for a heroic effort on the part of the community to save it. A historic preservation society of citizens called "Save the Scott House" (at the time it was known as the Scott house) formed in order to save the place from demolition. In 1976, after many ups and downs they finally raised the needed funds, all $375,000, to begin restoring the place to its former glory. Now the property is maintained by the Texas Heritage Corporation, Inc., and is open for public tours on Mondays, Wednesdays, and Fridays from 11 a.m. to 2 p.m., as well as Sundays from 1 to 3 p.m.

Some of the first indications that something was amiss in the house occurred during the period of these later renovations. Workers often felt uneasy when left alone in the house and some outright quit after reporting mysterious music emanating from the sealed off, third-floor ballroom. The work progressed nonetheless, and afterwards volunteers working in the house began to see two different apparitions. The first is of a woman dressed completely in white, which appears as if from thin air on the landing of the grand staircase; the second is of a man in a tennis outfit and a long, handlebar moustache, who is sometimes seen looking down from the top of the stairs.

Although neither of these phantoms has been known to interact with those witnessing them, the stories did draw the attention of local ghost hunters. On October 3, 1997, a group of ghost hunters and reporters spent the night in Thistle Hill hoping to find evidence of paranormal activity. After approximately eight hours in the place they may have gotten more than they bargained for. One of the first incidents during the investigation centered on a file of newspaper clippings and a flashlight that disappeared from a downstairs table. Later in the evening they would be found in the upstairs billiard room with no explanation as to how they arrived there. As the night progressed the group split up into teams of four to better cover all three floors. The team sweeping through the first floor with their flashlights and cameras later reported the sounds of footsteps and heavy objects being moved around on the floors above them. Teams already on the upper floors investigated the sounds, but were unable to find their source. Those on the second floor later claimed that they also heard voices coming from the veranda when it was empty. They were unable to make out the words themselves, but the sound was distinct enough to draw their attention.

The paranormal milestone of the evening however, centered on a 97-year-old rocking chair in the third floor ballroom; well known as a possible hot spot for activity. While combing the third floor, one team noticed the rocking chair had recently been turned to face the center of the ballroom. Further, the protective, plastic covering once draped over it, was now lying discarded on the floor. The ghost hunters placed the chair back into its original position and re-covered it with the plastic. Around 12 a.m., while making their rounds, they found to their surprise that the chair was again back to facing the dance floor with the plastic cover once more lying on the ground.

Back on the second floor, one of the ghost hunters had fallen asleep at their post and awoke with a start to find a dark, shapeless object hovering over her. As soon as she turned her flashlight on, the vaporous phantom disappeared back into the shadows from which it came. About now the investigation was wrapping up and although the phantoms of the house had so far avoided appearing in any photographs, they had made their presence known to the ghost hunters in other ways. As the group was packing up their equipment and leaving, they later swore that they heard the sound of a rocking chair creaking back and forth on the floors above.

Do the phantoms of a bygone era still roam the dark corridors of Thistle Hill or perhaps dance the night away in the old ballroom? We may never truly know. One thing we can be certain of however, the "Castle of Cowtown," still has a few secrets within its walls.

Thistle Hill Mansion, 1509 Pennsylvania Avenue, Fort Worth, Texas 76104
Web: www.thistlehill.org

The Haunted House Next Door

*"I saw it in the daylight, with the sun upon it.
There was no wind, no rain, no lightening, no
thunder, and no awful or unwonted circumstance,
of any kind, to heighten its effect."*
- Charles Dickens, *The Haunted House*

When most of us think about haunted houses we
often conjure up images of ancient structures with broken windows, creaky floorboards, and dark cobwebby
hallways. Most likely the image is a scene right out of
Hitchcock's *Psycho* or even an episode of the *Adams
Family*, complete with a full moon and the sounds
of wolves howling in the background. If we followed
the logic of Hollywood, this would indeed be sound
reasoning, but truth be told, ghosts can be found in
some of the most unassuming places. Take the case
of the Schoonover house for example; by all accounts
the Victorian-style home on Eighth Street is like any
of the other fine buildings that boarder the busy lane.
In fact, if you were to chance by it on some fine Texas
day, its buff colored brick walls and curving front porch
might seem down right inviting. It's the kind of place
you pass by on your way to work without giving it much
thought, or even the very house right next door. For all
its quaintness however, there are some who paint a

Schoonover Mansion.

different picture of the Schoonover house. Some would even go so far as to claim that despite its unobtrusive exterior, it's a place that harbors a presence no longer of this world.

In its lifetime the Schoonover house has seen its share of owners come and go. Commissioned by a successful, if not demanding, jeweler named James Mitchell in 1907, the house reflects the affluence of the city's "Silk Stocking District" at the turn of the century. For its design Mitchell chose the leading architectural firm of Saguinet and Staats, who you'll remember was responsible for such works as Thistle Hill and just about every other tall building constructed in Fort Worth before 1930. Once completed, the house didn't remain in Mitchell's hands for long and was sold to Dr. Charles B. Simmons in 1920. The property changed owners once again in 1945, when Dr. Simmons transferred the house to his daughter Maurine and her husband Frank Schoonover. The Schoonover family went on to grow and prosper in their new home until 1979, giving it the name by which it is known today.

In an article that ran in the *Fort Worth Star-Telegram* on October 31, 1993, reporter Mary Rogers interviewed Maurine Schoonover Packard, one of the surviving family members, about the history of the house. During the conversation she revealed that the house she once knew and loved had seen several unfortunate deaths in its lifetime. The first included her grandmother Velma Simmons, who died of natural causes and the second belonged to her father's long-time secretary, Lorene DeLipsy. Lorene, she explained, had no family of her own to speak of and lived in a small room upstairs at the back of the house. She suffered from a painfully, crippled hip and eventually died in her small room from Hodgkin's disease. It was only after Lorene's death that unusual activity began occurring around the house. The most telling incident that Mrs. Packard recalls happened as the family was preparing to move out in 1979. Mrs. Packard had just finished packing barrels full of items and stacking them in the basement before moving on to other chores. When she returned a short time later she found the barrels were completely rearranged; a task no one else in the house admitted to.

In 1981, architect Fred Cauble and partners Larry Hoskins, John Esch, and Toby Harrah purchased the Schoonover house and began the process of converting the structure into office space. It was in the midst of the renovations that the house became plagued by a series of unexplainable events. One night Cauble was entertaining guests with a tour of his new office. As the group entered the darkened basement they were struck by a dank, overpowering smell, as if the lower level had been sealed off for a long time. Cauble immediately apologized to his guests and explained that the basement had never smelled this way before. As he groped for the light switch he suddenly felt a set of icy fingers on the back of his shoulders. Turning on the light, he was shocked to find no one behind him. On another occasion Cauble was moving boxes by himself into a room at the head of the stairs. At one time it had been a sitting room, but was now destined to become his personal office. Struggling with a weighty box in both arms he bent forward to open a door that was shut tight. To his amazement he watched as the handle slowly turned and the door opened unassisted. At other times, items of importance seem to disappear mysteriously. The most common involved a roll of architectural plans that vanished periodically, only to be found the next day sitting on his desk in plain sight. His most bizarre experience however, occurred while working late into the night. Overwhelmed with project plans, Cauble sat with his nose buried in his work when he suddenly heard the sounds of a piano playing from the floor above. He was sure there was no piano in the house and as he rose to investigate, the lights flickered on and off frantically. When he reached the top of the stairs both the music and the light show stopped immediately.

Cauble wouldn't be the only person to run into something they couldn't account for while alone in the house. An architect named Bill Pruett was helping renovate the attic one evening when an orb of light about the size of a softball appeared. It zipped from one side of the attic to another as if threatening him. Pruett later reported that he made a decision to leave right then and there; doing so with the feeling that something was telling him he was unwelcome in the place.

Another visitor to the house who realized she was in over her head was a real estate agent named Trish

Brown. Mrs. Brown had heard some of Fred Cauble's stories about the place and was determined to find out the truth for herself. Exploring the basement one day, she felt an unnatural presence fill the room and a weight settle on her shoulders as if something were trying to drag her down. She quickly ran up the stairs and out the front door. Although she returned several times after, she never again experienced anything unusual.

In 1990, the house again saw new tenants, including a cosmetologist named Charlene Jones, who ran a salon from the top floor, and a plastic surgeon named Dr. Roger Harman, who leased office space on the ground level. In the meantime, the basement became an advertising firm named Marketing Relations, Inc., partnered by Denise Russell and Jerry Gladys. A might crowded you could say and I guess the ghosts of the Schoonover house thought so to, because little time passed before Charlene Jones moved out. Of the reasons she gave included the fact that she just couldn't keep her bottles of nail polish and shampoo from continually falling off the shelves.

Dr. Harman's office wouldn't go unscathed either and a rash of unusual activity began taking place on the first floor clinic. It was often the practice of the staff to set the thermostat at seventy degrees when leaving for the night, yet time and again when they returned the next day, they found it reset at eighty degrees. Becoming annoyed with the situation, Dr. Harman set the thermostat himself one night and placed a section of tape across the switch to prevent its movement. The next morning when he entered the office he discovered the heat turned right back up and the tape peeled back.

This of course did not mark the end of the activity but rather the start, as lights flickered on and off, important patient files disappeared, and strange noises sounded throughout the house. During all of this an apparition was sighted a number of times passing by the windows that looked out onto the street. In each case it was described as a man in a dark suit or rather the shadow of a man; no one could decide. Each time it was glimpsed out of the corner of the witness's eye making any detailed identification impossible.

There was one perk to working in a haunted house that the staff of the clinic could appreciate though. It seemed that despite a lot of rather unnerving activity on the part of the spirit, it did exhibit something of a fondness for plants. When the staff entered each morning it was not uncommon to find all of the plants in the reception room freshly watered, sometimes to the point of overflowing. Dr. Harman continued to experience paranormal activity until the day he finally moved his practice elsewhere.

Today the Schoonover house is owned and operated by the Art Brender Law Firm, who, understandably, doesn't take kindly to nosy writers like me snooping around during business hours. The fact remains that regardless of who inhabits the old house on Eighth Street, there is something amiss inside its walls. So be careful about the house down the street or perhaps even the one right next to yours; underneath its bright happy exterior, there's no telling what lurks inside. After all, you cannot always tell a house by its cover.

The Schoonover Mansion, 600 South Eighth Avenue, Fort Worth, Texas 76104

The Singing Ghost of Mistletoe Heights

"Often she sings! The melody is not recognizable,
and sometimes it sounds more like a hum,
or even a moan."
　　　- Docia Williams, *Phantoms of the Plains*

One of the more intriguing stories to come my way involves no ordinary, run of the mill phantom who occasionally steps from the shadows to say "boo," but one that's said to be able to actually carry a tune. When I first came to Texas one of the many tales to inspire my imagination centered on a ghost named Mattie, who was thought to haunt a house in the Mistletoe Heights area of Fort Worth. For days I scoured the area rumored to contain the haunted house. Up and down streets I wandered until my poor feet were just about to give out on me. Ghost hunting I would learn was not always a thrilling adventure; sometimes it took a lot of hard work. Part of the problem lay in the sources of the legend itself. Either those I interviewed were getting their information second hand or they tactfully refused to provide the address because it was a private residence. This would be no easy task to say the least and one that was shaping up to test my investigative skills to their fullest. Eventually, through a combination of luck and hours spent digging through the stacks of the local library, I managed to track the place down.

Haunted Mistletoe Heights home.

Mistletoe Heights is a neighborhood that sits on the bluffs overlooking the Clear Fork of the Trinity River just two miles south of Fort Worth's downtown. Many of the homes in the area have played a significant role in the city's history and have come to find their way into the Tarrant County Historical Society as registered landmarks. Set along wide, oak-lined streets flanked with ornamental streetlights, many of the structures range anywhere from clean-lined prairie bungalows, to handsome Tudor mansions.

The house we're most concerned with once belonged to Harry Hicks, president of the King Midas Oil and Gas Association, Ltd., who built the place along with his wife Sophrenia in 1920. Created in the sophisticated prairie style with its horizontal lines of plaster and wood, open interior spaces, and large porte-cochere, the house has seen many masters in its time. Although Harry Hicks was the first to live in the house, he sold it after only nine months to a D. J. Leahy. The house then passed through a long series of proprietors, some lasting a mere three months. Finally, in the 1950s, a family who resided there for almost three decades bought it.

The stories of the singing ghost first appeared in the late 1970s, with a woman named Barbara Doop, who was dating the owner of the Hicks house at the time (they later married and lived together in the home). One night over a romantic, candlelit dinner she noticed a movement across the room just beyond a set of French doors. Straining her eyes in the dim light Barbara spied the figure of a woman on the other side of the doors with her head bent down as if listening intently. She had light, brown hair fashioned in a Gibson girl roll common in the Victorian era and striking blue eyes with white, porcelain skin, and a high collared blouse and brooch. From that night forward the phantom was affectionately known as Mattie.

Over the next thirty-five years Mattie continued to appear to various owners of the house, all of who described her in much the same way as Barbara Doop. Many also noticed that she tended to frequent the staircase that ran from the basement to the pantry. In fact, so common were her appearances in this location that the pantry became something of a paranormal hot spot in the home. Unexplained sounds originated from it, including odd thumps and bangs so loud they reverberated throughout the rest of the house. One family reported first hand the startling nature of the sounds. While sitting down to dinner one evening a loud, crashing sound exploded from the pantry as if a car had just driven through the wall of the house. Rushing to the source of the horrendous sound, they threw open the pantry doors only to find nothing out of place. Mattie could also express her disapproval in other unsettling ways when she felt the pantry area was being threatened. In one case, a previous owner awoke from a pleasant sleep to find the ghostly figure of Mattie floating above the bed. It seems that the phantom was upset about some items that were taken from the pantry and wanted them returned immediately. The next day, shaken by the angry apparition, the owner quickly restocked the pantry with the missing items. This evidently did the trick because Mattie refrained from making any further nightly visits.

The tale of the phantom's love for song however didn't gain prominence until the 1980s, when owners of the house granted permission to ghost hunters, Terry Smith and Mark Jean, to conduct an investigation. Using a combination of high tech equipment and the abilities of psychic Elaine Gibbs, the team filmed a series of seances in the home over a period of five nights. On July 11, 1987, while attempting to contact the spirit, the film crew heard the sounds of soft, melodic humming fill the air. The distinctive sound was an unfamiliar tune and none of the ghost hunters could agree on which direction it emanated from. A later review of their recording equipment proved futile as well, due to the fact that the ghostly sounds failed to register on any of their instruments.

In time others would come for the chance to hear Mattie hum the lost refrain. One psychic traveled from as far as California to speak with Mattie, claiming that he was led to the house by a series of dreams. After several hours alone in a room he emerged and described communicating with a spirit that matched the description of Mattie provided by earlier residents. She was, he went on to say, attached to the house and was by no means leaving. Since then Mattie seems to have lost her voice and current owners report that they haven't heard a peep out of her since they moved in. The only oddity in the house is an occasional shadow in the hallway that sometimes moves about without blending into any of the others.

I thought a lot about whether or not it would be proper to disclose the location of the Hicks house in Mistletoe Heights. After all, I did search long and hard to finally track the place down. Then I thought better of it and like those before me, I opted to keep its exact whereabouts a secret. The Hicks house is still someone's home and I doubt they or even Mattie for that matter would appreciate being inundated with curiosity seekers. If you're still intent on finding the place for yourself then this is what I suggest. Find a nice place to park your car and then comb the streets of Mistletoes Heights on foot, it's well worth the exercise. Then, as it grows dark and the ornate lampposts flicker on one by one, listen for the sound of the wind through the leaves of the tall Oaks. If you listen hard enough you might just hear a gentle melody pass by in the voice of a woman who no longer lives on this earth.

The Mistletoe Heights House,
Private Residence, Location Undisclosed

Gussie's House

"I think at first she was here to remind me that this is her house." - Jim Lane

Sometimes it's easy to get caught up in all of the moaning and chain rattling when you're listening to a good Texas ghost story. Why if the storyteller knows half of what they're doing they can have the hairs on the back of your neck standing on end and your eyes darting to every slinking shadow that fills the room. You can even forget the fact that the characters, which inhabit these tales, were once flesh and blood people just like you or I. They lived lives encompassing all of the joys and sorrows that go to make up the human drama we call life. The next tale is no exception and contains all of the elements found in the human condition—a bittersweet tale of love, sacrifice, and loneliness. You see, to say that Augusta "Gussie" Armstrong loved her house would be an understatement, because it seems that even death couldn't keep her from coming back home.

Perched atop the bluffs overlooking the Trinity River, the Armstrong house sits tucked away in a corner of Grand Avenue just as the street makes a sloping turn and continues north. Built in 1906, in the post-Victorian style so popular at the time, the

The Armstrong house.

box-like two-story affair with its simple rounded columns and dormer window set into the roof affords a breathtaking view of the river bottoms. It takes no stretch of the imagination to see why Gussie fell in love with the place, but to understand just what she gave up for it requires a little more reading.

W. L. Armstrong, whose portrait still hangs in the parlor, in his confederate uniform, was living in the small town of Rising Star with his wife and six children. When Mrs. Armstrong succumbed to tuberculosis and died, Gussie was 21-years-old and, for the beautiful, young woman engaged to be married, life would take an unexpected turn. According to the *Armstrongs of the Catawba*, a 1969 genealogy by Norma Todd Cansler, after the death of his wife Mr. Armstrong asked Gussie to break off her engagement and move from Cisco to Fort Worth in order to take care of the family. In return, he offered to build her the house of her dreams. It couldn't have been an easy choice to make, but in the end she agreed to her father's request. For the rest of her life Gussie devoted herself to raising her younger siblings, watching them grow and eventually move away to start families of their own. She never did come close to marriage again and, when her father died in 1923, she was left all alone in that big house on the hill.

The house, for which she had given up so much, was all that she knew now and she seldom left it. Instead, she preferred to spend her time writing letters to her nieces and nephews and keeping up the house.

When she became too old and stiff to transverse the stairs, a kitchen was installed on the second floor next to her bedroom. In 1954, at the age of 75, Gussie Armstrong died alone in the house and since that time it has become the center of a whirlwind of paranormal activity. She often appears around the house, followed by dramatic temperature drops and the scent of fresh cut flowers. Although she seems to welcome men, even becoming flirtatious at times, she can be down right hostile when another woman enters her home. In the 1960s, the activity became so frequent that the Catholic church was asked to step in by the owners and rid the house of its spirit. However, after repeated attempts to exorcise the ghost the priest ended with a note that the spirit would not be budged. It seemed that Gussie was here to stay.

When City Councilman and attorney, Jim Lane, first saw the house, like Gussie he fell in love with the place at first sight. A bachelor who lived alone, he put a lot of work into restoring the place to its former condition, including going to such lengths as to match the original paint colors and fill it with old photographs and antiques. Jim's first encounter with Gussie happened one night while he lay in the upstairs bedroom reading with his gray cat Higby nestled against him. Hearing a rustling sound he looked up from his book to find a beautiful woman standing in the doorway. Placing her hand against the doorframe she gave him what he would later describe as "a very provocative" look before floating away. She was dressed in a diaphanous garment of white with dark flowing hair and large brown eyes. Although Gussie died at a ripe old age, Jim thinks that she chooses to return looking like she did when she was much younger. Over time Jim ran into the spirit of Gussie on a number of occasions and not once has he felt threatened by her. To the contrary, he feels like she returns to make sure her house is still in order. That and he thinks she may have a bit of a crush on him.

Jim isn't the only one to witness the ghost of Gussie Armstrong. When he first bought the residence his mother and father came over to see the new place. As they approached the house they climbed the front steps and, peering through the glass paneled door, noticed a dark haired woman in white standing in the dining room. Thinking it might be a friend of their son's, they entered only to find the place empty. One of the more harrowing incidents however, transpired while Jim was traveling through Europe. While away two Fort Worth police officers was house-sitting for him. The arrangement didn't last long though and upon his return he found that both had experienced the phantom of the house. Neither would elaborate on their encounter, but one man fled the house during the middle of his second night there in nothing more than his underwear. Even the next day he refused to enter the house to retrieve his clothes.

In October of 1995, journalists from the *Fort Worth Star-Telegram* were granted permission to spend the night in the house and conduct a little ghost hunt of their own. They began the evening by spreading fresh rose petals in the rooms she is most thought to frequent: the first floor music room and the second floor bedrooms. A bit of ghost bait they surmised, given her love of floral scents. Around midnight the group split up into smaller teams with each assigned to monitor a different room. It didn't take long, and about an hour after they settled in, investigators in the music room felt the temperature drop and the hair on their arms and neck stand on end. By now one of the female investigators felt so overwhelmed by a constant impression of unwelcome that she demanded to leave the house. Soon after, two other ghost hunters witnessed a vague, gray blob float approximately two feet above the level of the stairs. It was like nothing they had seen before. It shimmered like the surface of water. By five in the morning the last of the team had fallen asleep in their sleeping bags. The ghost hunt was over.

Jim Lane would go on to continue reporting sightings of the apparition that roamed through the house. In addition to the manifestations mentioned above she seemed to like moving heavy furniture around when no one was present and on one occasion Jim swears she even took the trash out. Gussie Armstrong gave up a tremendous amount in her life for the welfare of her family and after they were gone all she had was the house. Perhaps the house, her house, was the only thing she knew anymore; the only source of happiness in a life devoted to others. Either way, regardless of who has occupied the place over the years, it has only ever belonged to Gussie. Jim Lane will tell you that although he lives there, he's just the custodian. This is really Gussie's house.

Like the home in Mistletoe Heights this is a private residence and the owners deserve their peace. Therefore I will refrain from listing the address.

The Armstrong House, Private Residence, Location Undisclosed

The Ghost of Seat 13

*"All the world is a stage
and all the men and women merely players:
they have their exits and their entrances."*
- William Shakespeare, *As You Like It*

The theater, with its lively pageantry and sweeping music has always attracted a crowd. Whether it's a billing of *Hamlet* or *Joseph and the Technicolor Dreamcoat*, everyone loves a good show. In some cases, however, not everyone filling the audience seats for a performance may be of the flesh and blood persuasion. There is a long history of stages the world over that proudly claims to be in possession of their very own ghost. These hauntings can range anywhere from long, dead thespians still intent on reciting their lines to ghostly spectators back from the grave to catch just one more act. As far back as Shakespeare or Donizetti, ghosts have always fired the imaginations of theatergoers. Gaston Lexor took full advantage of the legends when he opened *Phantom of the Opera*, with the characters excitedly claiming to have seen a ghost haunting the opera house. Not to be outdone, Fort Worth has its own story to tell of a phantom haunting the auditorium of Nicholas Martin Hall, on the campus of Texas Wesleyan University.

Texas Wesleyan University was founded in 1890 by the Methodist Episcopal Church as an institution of higher learning and to promote the spread of Southern Methodism. A site was chosen just east of the city on land donated by a number of early pioneer families. Originally the fledgling school was named Polytechnic College, which literally means, "many arts and sciences." The first classes began in 1891 with only a handful of faculty and 111 eager young students. By 1914, with restructuring of the church's educational program, the campus became an all girls' institution and was aptly named Texas Women's College. As the new college grew in size and recognition, young women from all over Texas flocked to its educational programs, making it the leading women's institution in North Texas. In fact, it remained such until the economic constraints of the Great Depression forced it to merge with Texas Wesleyan Academy in Austin and incorporate men into the student body once again. Time went by and the campus continued to expand, extending its boundaries into the surrounding neighborhoods springing up around it. Although it's now an institution that welcomes individuals from all faiths, it continues to maintain the comprehensive academic excellence that made it one of Texas's finest liberal arts colleges. By 1989, it expanded its curriculum and facilities to achieve the dream under which it was first conceived—to become a university.

On the southeast side of the campus, with its grassy lawns and limestone brick structures, sits the Ann Waggoner Fine Arts Building. After numerous enlargements

Entrance to the Ann Waggoner Fine Arts Building.

and extensive remodeling, the building now houses teaching studios, rehearsal rooms, an electronic piano laboratory, and a theater—the Nicholas Martin Performance Hall. In addition, the old building has also become the stage for a ghostly legend passed around by students and professors alike. According to campus rumors, the fine arts building occupies land once set aside for an old stone church and cemetery in 1908. The bodies interned in the soil were never removed during the construction as a simple matter of convenience. One of those forgotten graves is said to have belonged to a woman named Georgia, who was a great lover of music when she was alive. Now, with her resting place disturbed, she rises each night to haunt the theater.

As theatrical as the story sounds, upon closer inspection we find that like many enduring legends this one carries in it a seed of truth. Interestingly enough, the building does sit immediately adjacent to grounds once used as a burial plot for Dr. W.C. Dobkins and his family. Dr. Dobkins was known to be the school's first resident physician. When the land came under development by the growing college, all but three graves were exhumed and relocated to others burial grounds. Why these three were left untouched is a bit of mystery itself. All we do know is that they belonged to Dr. Dobkins late sister, Sarah, buried in 1896, followed by a young boy named Joe in 1897, and an infant who died one day after birth in 1898. We cannot be for sure which way Sarah's musical tastes ran, but we do know that she was physically handicapped and never married.

By the time the first sighting of the phantom was recorded late one night in 1955, during a rehearsal of the musical *Brigadoon*, her story was already well known. The late Mason Johnson, head of the drama department and professor emeritus of theater arts, was preparing for the musical's opening when he first encountered the specter. Sitting in the audience section taking notes while the cast performed, he began to get the creepy sensation that someone was watching him. He then noticed for the first time that a woman was seated in the audience slightly forward of his position and to the right in one of the aisle seats. The rehearsal was closed to the public and so the presence of an intruder in the auditorium annoyed him enough that he was determined to discover exactly what business she had being there. Standing up, Professor Johnson started down the aisle towards the figure, but just before he reached her seat she vanished into thin air. Worried that he might be hallucinating, he resumed his seat only to find that when he looked over the woman was back in her seat again. For awhile he simply sat there staring at the woman as she intently watched the actors on the stage. Finally, unable to stand it any longer, he rose from his seat and started down the aisle towards the figure only to find that once again she disappeared, right before his eyes. From that point on he began referring to her as Georgia. He doesn't know why the name came to him, only that it seemed to fit the ghost perfectly; either way the name stuck.

Since that night many others have reported witnessing the phantom figure of Georgia and remarkably they often describe her in much the same way. She appears as a grayish mist with a definite outline and features, wearing a Victorian dress from the 1890s, with puffed sleeves, bodice, and a brooch ending at a high collar and shawl. Most think that she's an older woman around sixty, with grayish hair parted down the middle and pulled into a bun at the back of the neck. A good deal of the time she can be found sitting in her favorite seat (number 13), but at other times she is said to glide back and forth across the upper balconies; the sound of her tread the only evidence of her passing. She also seems to have a great affection for musicals involving dance sections with lively tunes and loves to pop in most during their rehearsals. Some of her favorites are noted to be *South Pacific*, *Kiss Me Kate*, *Carousel*, *Cabaret*, *Gypsy*, and *Fiddler on the Roof*.

Professor Johnson encountered the phantom many times during his tenure at the theater. Another memorable incident occurred during a rehearsal of the musical *Cabaret*. The cast had just finished and Professor Johnson was turning off the lights when he looked out into the darkened auditorium and spied the ghost of Georgia sitting in her favorite seat. Dashing backstage, he rounded up his students and brought them out to see the ghost for themselves. Quietly, so as not to spook the old gal, they filed onto the stage and watched, as the ghost remained visible for sometime. There she sat, staring back at them just as all the stories said she

Georgia's seat.

would. She—a gray, misty phantom, sitting like a statue, they—a gaggle of dumbstruck students.

In 2002, the Nicholas Martin Performance Hall received an extensive remodeling, at the cost of two million dollars. In order to recognize the theater's greatest and in this case, oldest fan, President Harold Jeffcoat approved a plan designed to add to her posterity. All the seats in the auditorium were upholstered in navy blue with the exception of one, seat 13. As the theater program at Texas Wesleyan University continues to perform great dramatical works, you can be sure that Georgia or whatever her name really happens to be, is right there watching the show. In fact the theater program has adopted her as something of a good luck charm. Whenever she appears at a rehearsal, it's believed, the show is guaranteed to be a hit.

---

*Texas Wesleyan University, Nicholas Martin Hall,
Ann Waggoner Fine Arts Building,
1309 Wesleyan Street, Fort Worth, Texas 76105*

Bird's Fort

"Old soldiers never die; they just fade away."
- Douglas MacArthur

It was a balmy day in June when I received a call from ghost hunters Carl Hullett and Les Ramesdale, inviting me to join them on an investigation of a site that once contained an old military outpost known as Bird's Fort. Having worked with these two ghost hunters in the past at locations such as Carter, I knew that before the evening was finished I was in for a real treat. Scribbling down the directions Carl gave me, I hung up the phone and grabbed my best pair of boots, and some fresh batteries, a trusty flashlight, and the always important can of bug spray. Now, I told myself, I was ready for just about anything.

A quick glance at the map revealed that Bird's Fort lay nestled in the cradle of a bow shaped lake just east of the city, on a patch of field surrounded by housing developments. Traveling down Interstate 30 towards Arlington, it was hard to imagine how the countryside first looked to the pioneers making their way across the expanse with their entire lives loaded into an oxcart. The sight of those gently, rolling fields of tall grass interspersed by thick clumps of oak and hickory, while bubbling streams fed hackberries and

Site once occupied by Bird's Fort.

pecan trees in their alluvial sediment, must have cut quite the picture. If the early settlers found the land to be a place of beauty; then they also found it to be a place of hardship. Much to their consternation they also found it already occupied by Native American tribes such as the Wichita and Caddoan, people that had lived there for hundreds of years, spread across the prairie in domed grass huts, hunting buffalo and raising corn. Unfortunately the meeting of these two cultures would be anything but amicable and instead, led to a long series of atrocities and suffering for both sides. Today of course neither side would recognize the land they lived and died for. The gated communities, strip malls, and congested highways that mark modern day man's progress has replaced all of the pastoral landmarks that made the land what it was.

Taking the Collins Street exit I veered north until I stumbled across Trinity Boulevard and then east until the crowded sections of the city grew thinner. Turning south again along Euless Main, I continued for several miles until the housing complexes began to fade and the road became a rough dirt track. Once again I was amazed at just how in the world these two ghost hunters found such a secluded location in the first place. Eventually, after splashing through numerous deep ruts, the road ended abruptly next to a rain-swollen lake surrounded by a patchwork of oak and mesquite. Evening was just over the horizon when I arrived and found Carl and Les patiently waiting for me. After a hearty welcome and some more good-natured ribbing about ghost cows, we began unloading the ghost tracking equipment we would use during the investigation. As the rest of the team positioned the video cameras and night vision optics, I took the opportunity to look around the area. Sadly, nothing remains of the outpost itself, but a graffiti stained historical marker jutting from the ground. The only other evidence of human occupation consists of several dilapidated structures belonging to more recent attempts to establish a resort next to the lake. However, like every other endeavor to settle the area, it too failed and was abandoned.

Major Jonathon Bird and the 4th Brigade of Texas Militia, under the orders of General Edwards H. Tarrant, of the Republic of Texas, constructed Bird's Fort in 1841. The garrisoning of such an outpost in hostile Indian Territory was an attempt to attract settlers, most of who came from the Red River area, with the promise of military protection—a promise they would later learn was easier said than done. Initially it consisted of a wooden stockade and trench encircling a series of blockhouses and smaller homes. As time went by and greater numbers of settlers flocked to the outpost, additional homes sprang up outside the walls.

Even before the fort was erected the land had seen its share of bloodshed. On May 24, 1841, the Republic of Texas Militia engaged three Indian tribes-the Caddos, Cherokees, and Tonkawas-in a fierce battle that left bodies from both sides littering the

Bird's Fort historical marker.

ground as it waged back and forth. Incidents such as these only proved to heighten tensions between the Anglos and the Indians, laying the seeds for the small outpost's failure. Through costly experience the Indians came to find that they could not face regular troops in open battle and so took to fighting a gorilla war against the settlers and their newly built fort. One tactic they employed was to burn the grass and other cover surrounding the fort. This scorched earth policy forced the fort's hunting parties farther away from its protective walls where they could be ambushed more easily. Persistent attacks, combined with chronic supply shortages, and failed farming attempts would eventually lead to the fort's abandonment in 1842. Life at the tiny outpost proved to be just too hard for settlers and soldiers alike, and the ground around it came to claim many. It's unknown just how many are buried there, but one section is known to contain the bodies of two men and a little girl killed in an ambush while fetching water from the lake.

The fort continued to sit empty for a year before gaining a brief bit of life when two important events thrust it back into history. The first occurred in August of 1843, when the "Band of Invincibles," under Jacob Snivley, disbanded at the fort after raiding Mexican gold shipments along the Santa Fe Trail. Of course the raiders didn't quit the hunt voluntarily, but only under the forced supervision of the U.S. Army and not a trace of the legendary gold was ever recovered. The second event transpired just one month later on

September 29, 1843, when Generals G.W. Terrell and E.H. Tarrant met at the fort with ten Indian tribes to sign the treaty of Bird's Fort. This piece of paper ended the hostilities and established a short-lived border between Indian land and territory open for settlement. After this last bit of posterity the fort fell into ruins and disappeared back into the landscape it sprang from, a mere footnote in the pages of Texas history.

With the equipment ready we outlined a search perimeter using aerial photographs of the site and began sweeping the area for paranormal activity. That gave us a chance to discuss some of the stories associated with the place, as we struggled through flooded marsh and forest trails. Many visitors to the area report phantom figures out of the corner of their eyes, as well as the sound of voices at night that seem to rise up from the very ground. One of the more popular stories involves a stubborn canine that wouldn't leave his master even in death. One day a hunter named Wade Rattan was ambushed and killed by a raiding party of Indian braves. When the search party from the fort stumbled across his arrow-ridden corpse, they also found his loyal bulldog alive and guarding the body. Days later when the body of Wade was laid to rest just 200 yards from the fort, it was said that his dog just sat there watching the proceedings. After the burial nothing more is said about the faithful dog, but some visitors to the site today claim to hear his lonely howling at night. All attempts to locate the animal drives it farther away, always just out of reach.

Another ghostly tale linked to the fort concerns the phantom of an Indian chief in full battle dress that roams the site still seeking revenge against the white man that murdered his family. His story is said to take place one day in 1842, when a lone rider, named Simon Trask, entered the camp. Like any hard riding cowboy the first thing Trask did when he hit the place was head straight for the makeshift saloon, where he began to drink heavily and boast about his Indian fighting exploits. The more he drank, the louder he got, until he ended his drunken tirade with a disturbing story. Recently, he claimed, he ambushed a local Wichita chief and raped his wife and daughter before killing all three. As Trask's terrible story drew to a close he seemed to have reached his limit and so stumbled off to the pleasure tent with a young, working girl named Beth Ann.

Most of the patrons were just happy to be rid of the troublemaker and so returned to their drinking when a scream pierced the air from the direction of the pleasure tent. Pouring into the tent the men stopped short at a scene so grisly even the hardest became faint at heart. Trask lay dead on the tent floor with his throat cut and his body resembling a pincushion full of arrows. The hysterical Beth Ann lay crouched in the corner repeating over and over that the ghost of an Indian in war paint and feathers had murdered Trask. The body was quickly buried by the fort's work detail with little ceremony. Men like Trask were despised for the trouble they stirred up as they passed through, often leaving the poor settlers to clean up their mess. Beth Ann later came to her senses and elaborated on the frightening events of that night. Once she and Trask had entered the tent, she told listeners, he began to beat her mercilessly and pulling his knife from his belt threatened to cut her throat. During the assault a light appeared behind him and began to form into the shape of an Indian covered in blood and war paint. Arrows suddenly flew into Trask's body as if from nowhere as the phantom Indian pulled out his knife and scalped the dying man. The lighted figure then disappeared just as Beth Ann started to scream. Despite its ferocity however, Beth Ann claimed that neither phantom nor man made a single sound during the struggle. Since that time, legend states that whenever a woman is in trouble near the site, the gruesome figure of an Indian will appear to scare off her attacker.

Around 3 a.m., we finally tired and began collecting the equipment. Admittedly we had seen little more than a pickup truck full of teenagers who drove off in fright at the sight of us. Later photographic evidence revealed some strange lights in the pictures. One shows a dark forested trail with a line of phantom-like lights marching by as if they were soldiers on patrol. Perhaps the spirits here have returned to replay old battles or settle old scores. Maybe for them the fight continues, long after the sounds of the guns have stopped and the stockade walls have vanished. As the housing complexes march closer, hemming the spot on each side, one thing is for certain: someday even this place of history will vanish beneath progress.

Bird's Fort: take FM 157 one mile north of the Trinity River in Arlington, Texas

---

The Curse of "Death's Crossing"

*Legend has it that if you go to the bridge at night
you can hear screaming ghosts.*
- Fort Worth Star-Telegram

Northeast of the city runs a lonely stretch of dirt
track hemmed by thorny briars and twisted mesquite
trees known as the Arlington-Bedford Road. Once
called "Old Harrison Road," it crosses a set of railroad tracks at a spot some believe may be one of Fort
Worth's most haunted locations. Even during the day,
while traveling down the narrow roadway, you get the
sense that something's out of place. Perhaps it's the
stillness of the air that hangs heavier here or the lack
of background noise from birds and insects, either way
there's an odd quality to it. For years the crossing has
been shunned as a place haunted by past tragedies; a
cursed place that the locals believe "occasionally takes
someone." Yet for others, including local ghost hunters,
it's a place filled with unexplained activity they believe
is linked to the spirits of those who have died here.
Today the locale is known as "Death's Crossing," but
over time it has come to collect a wide assortment of
ghastly names, designed no doubt by area teenagers
looking to scare one another. Although the stories associated with the crossing are as fanciful as any of the

Lonely road leading to "Death's Crossing."

best urban legends modern storytellers have to offer, the truth of the matter is, the terrible events that have transpired here are frighteningly real.

Many of the legends surrounding the location stem from a fatal car accident in the 1960s. At the time the area was reputedly known as "Screaming Bridge," due to a narrow wooden overpass that spanned a section of the road. Teenagers out for a joyride raced their cars across the rickety, old structure late at night, causing the timbers to groan loudly under the weight of their vehicles. Add to this a few well-worked tales of screaming ghosts lurking around the bridge and you're guaranteed a good scare for everyone.

However, "Screaming Bridge" represented more than just a source of entertainment for local youths—it was also a symbol of sorts. On the other side of the bridge lay a 40-foot ravine crossed by a second bridge and then a set of railroad tracks leading to a cut of bottomland known as Mosier Valley. This literally marked the other side of the tracks for many and acted as a dividing line between the black and white communities. Many of the residents of Mosier Valley were descendents of freed slaves from the old Mosier Plantation, who after their emancipation formed a tight-knit farming community in the 1870s. Relations between the two communities were never good at best, and as the era of the civil rights movement approached the south, they only got worse. As the nation struggled over the issue of equality for all men, smaller communities like Mosier Valley boiled over with tension. One night in

1960, white youths burned the second bridge in an act of vandalism designed to separate the communities even further. When the rail line discovered the damage they erected barricades and posted signs notifying motorists of the danger. In a further act of destruction, the warning signs were then stolen, setting the stage for the tragedy about to befall.

It happened at approximately 10 p.m. on a cold February evening in 1961. The night was foggy and a light, misty rain filled the air, reducing visibility to a mere few feet. Bill Young, a high school student at the time, was traveling down the isolated road with his date that night when he stopped at the bridge to let a train pass. It was in the light of the speeding locomotive that he first noticed something was wrong. Stepping from his car he was shocked to find the bridge out and the front wheels of his car barely two feet from the drop off. Turning the car around, he drove south again as another vehicle passed him heading for the bridge. In an attempt to warn the vehicle, Bill Young sounded his horn and flashed his lights. The intended warning, however, seemed to have the opposite affect, as the car accelerated even faster, barreling through the barricades, and crashing into the opposite embankment. Braking the car Bill Young jumped out and ran to the bridge, but it was too late. All he could see through the fog was the flash of taillights below and a painful whimpering sound that rose from the darkness. Involved in the crash were six high school girls returning home from a movie in Fort Worth. The three seated in the front of the vehicle, Mary Lou Goldner, Claude Jean Reeves, and Kathy Fleming, were killed in the impact; the remaining three, all seated in the back, were badly injured and rushed off to area hospitals.

Four local high school boys later confessed to burning the bridge that resulted in the fatal accident and were expelled from school. Although a reward was offered for information leading to the arrest of those responsible for stealing the warning signs, no one was ever identified. To ensure the safety of future motorists the bridges were removed and replaced with a graded incline of earth and gravel. "Screaming Bridge" was no more, but even as it disappeared, its legend refused to, and the story found itself transferred to other area bridges.

As with any good story, many of the legends cropping up around "Death's Crossing" have become more fantastical with each passing generation. The first claims that if you stand on the bridge at midnight (remember it no longer exists) on the anniversary of the crash, glowing tombstones will rise from the water below. In a bit of added detail the grave markers are said to bare the names and dates of those killed in the crash. A similar version requires that you actually sit on the bridge at midnight, until a creepy fog rises to engulf the overpass. If you're brave enough to remain, headlights will appear in the fog moving toward you. Not to worry though because right before the moment of impact, they disappear, followed by the noise of a car crashing into the ravine below and the sounds of screams filling the darkness.

Another spooky tale linked to the crossing involves the supposed death of a hobo some years ago. No one seems to know the transient's name or the date of the murder, but few storytellers' chance ruining the tale by questioning its details. One night a hobo was sleeping next to the tracks when he heard the sounds of struggle and a woman's voice crying out for help. Stumbling onto the crossing he discovered a parked car containing a couple that seemed to be fighting. The hobo rushed to the woman's aid, but was shot during the ensuing struggle. The next day police found the woman wandering through the countryside in a state of shock and the body of the homeless man at the scene of the murder. Since his death, young lovers parking near the crossing at night have recounted seeing the ghost of a man in rags looking in through the window at them and tapping on the car door before vanishing in thin air.

On March 10, 1994, "Death's Crossing" furthered its sinister reputation by claiming the lives of yet two more young women. At the same spot as the accident thirty-three years previous, a Northern Burlington train struck a Ford pickup as it attempted to cross the tracks. The vehicle immediately burst into flames as the locomotive dragged it almost 900 feet before hurling it into a ravine. The two passengers, Rayelynn Johnston and Tammy Dodson, were pronounced dead at the scene. The details of the events leading up to their deaths are a bit of a mystery. The only thing for certain is that the crossing had again taken more innocent lives.

The infamous "Death's Crossing."

Determined to understand the phenomenon that was taking place at "Death's Crossing," ghost hunters and visitors alike have explored the site looking for clues. During many investigations, unexplained activity has appeared on film and audiotape. Some of the manifestations common to the site range from sudden drops in temperature to pulsating orbs of light. In the midst of one investigation involving a local news crew, a ghost hunter was being interviewed at the tracks when a ghostly voice could be heard in response to one of the reporter's questions. Later, captured by the news crew's sound equipment, it was replayed on a Halloween segment airing in 2005. On another ghost hunt, a psychic was brought in to communicate with the ghosts believed to haunt the crossing. Despite failed attempts to contact the spirits, the psychic did report the strong presence of two female entities hovering around the tracks.

The world over is full of various rivers, lakes, and mountains that have come to be called cursed by those that dwell near them; fearful landmarks that seem to draw tragedy to themselves time and again, as if feeding on the negative energy. Yet could "Death's Crossing" be such a place? For the answer I turned to Carl Hullett, now of DFW Ghost Hunters, and one of the leading experts on "Death's Crossing." Carl has studied the site for years and currently leads ghost tours of the crossing as well as many other haunted locations in Fort Worth. When I asked the all-important question of whether or not there was any basis for the legends, his response was simple.

"I don't think the place is cursed in the traditional sense of the term, but I sure do think it's haunted."

"Death's Crossing" is located along an old dirt road in the vicinity of Trinity Boulevard and Greenbelt Road.

The "Lost Cemetery of Infants"

"The lawn Is pressed by unseen feet,
and ghosts return gently at twilight,
gently go at dawn, the sad intangible who
grieve and yearn..."
   - T.S. Eliot, *To Walter de la Mare*

I first heard about the "Lost Cemetery of Infants" on the news one evening, while I was busy going over my notes on a previous case. The newswoman was recounting the chilling tale of a cemetery to the east of the city, filled it would seem entirely with the graves of infants. According to the newscast there was a legend that on nights when the moon was full and shining high overhead, the cries of the children buried there could be heard rising from the ground. She was sketchy on the location of the burial place (it was supposed to be the "lost" cemetery after all), but that didn't matter because I knew just the person to call on this one. Amy Wainwright of DFW Ghost Hunters has investigated haunted locations in and around Fort Worth for years. She is also known for her tireless efforts in helping others form groups of their own and experience the thrill of ghost hunting first hand. After contacting her I was relieved to find that she knew just the place I was talking about. Better yet, she agreed to meet me there and give me the grand tour.

Infant grave marker.

The "Lost Cemetery" sits huddled in a secluded corner of Doug Russell Park, adjacent to the University of Texas at Arlington. Its three acres of well-kept grounds lie covered in tall oak trees that look as if they could have been there for over a hundred years. Tucked into the northeast section of the park is a small cemetery surrounded by a cyclone fence and bordered on its northern edge by a shallow ravine and stream. It's easy to miss it if you're not sure what to look for because all but one of the weathered grave markers lie flat against the landscape in the form of tiny plaques.

The land first came under development in 1894 when the Reverend James Tony Upchurch founded the Berachah Industrial Home for the Redemption and Protection of Erring Girls on a slight knoll he called "Rescue Hill." The term Berachah comes from the Hebrew word for blessing and symbolized the hopes Rev. Upchurch had for the place. The program took expectant, unwed mothers and taught them a self-sustaining trade while living at the home, a step thought highly controversial for its age. In the early part of the century unwed, pregnant mothers were outcasts from society to be shunned by their community. Even many churches refused to help what they referred to as "fallen women." Although early records indicate that there were deep divisions between the home and nearby towns, nothing suggests that Rev. Upchurch and his girls were anything less than tolerated.

There were only three rules for the girls that came to Berachah: everyone worked, everyone attended Sunday worship, and children born in the home had to stay with their mother for at least one year. Rev. Upchurch was a firm believer that the welfare of the child rested in the care of the natural mother. Not all of the women who came to Berachah were with child however; some were runaways, heroin addicts, or simply widows without the means to support themselves. During the first seventeen years of its operations, records claim that over 1,100 women and children were admitted with 75 percent returning to what was considered an "honorable and useful life." The program became so popular that applications poured in from all over the country and each month some had to be turned down due to lack of space.

Berachah originally blanketed 27 acres and was formed with money earned from the women's industrial efforts, as well as donations from local businessmen. The home thrived under Rev. Upchurch's magnanimous care and by 1921, had transformed into a complex covering no less than 40 acres. The campus came to include a two-story girl's dormitory, a nursery capable of accommodating up to 35 newborns, a maternity hospital, contagious disease infirmary, and a gardener's quarters. To teach important life skills for reentry into society a laundry, print shop, and industrial buildings where the women learned to make handkerchiefs were added. Finally, but certainly not least in the eyes of Rev. Upchurch and his staff, the home boasted its own chapel for services and classes, as well as a 1,000 seat auditorium for meetings and concerts. The Berachah Home had become a tiny self-sustaining city of its own.

Given the size of the community and the less than stellar quality of medical care at the time, a number of children were delivered still-born or died from later complications; others fell victim to subsequent epidemics of influenza and measles, which swept through the area in 1914. To intern the tiny bodies a cemetery was created with the first burial taking place in 1904. Many of the infants buried here died before they were even given names and so their plaques simply read "Baby No. 1," and so on in orderly little rows. The remaining markers bare only first names in an attempt to protect the identity of the young mothers. To date the cemetery is estimated to contain as many as 80 graves, of which only a small portion is clearly marked.

Unfortunately, the work that Rev. Upchurch started ended with him as well. In 1935, the Berachah Home was sold due to Rev. Upchurch's deteriorating health and soon after ceased to exist. Rev. Upchurch later died on September 12, 1950. The living quarters and shops that came to occupy the grounds were torn down in the 1960s, as the land was parceled off and sold. The last remnant of Rev. Upchurch's great social endeavor was a small stone chapel that sat next to the cemetery grounds. In time it too was demolished when the university purchased the property, because vandals would periodically set fire to the building.

As Amy and I strolled through the park grounds, she was keen to point out some of the remaining foundation lines that represented the former buildings. They were difficult to discern at first and plain impossible if you weren't outright looking for them. In time, however, I began to develop a picture of the past and was impressed by the size of its dimensions. Although Amy and her team have yet to capture the sounds of ghostly infants crying out in the night, they have experienced manifestations of other kinds. During investigations of the site, team members have encountered the sounds of invisible footsteps following them around and have witnessed shadowy figures peeking out at them from around trees. On a number of occasions, ghost hunters have reported having their hair caressed by unseen hands while trying to set up their equipment. In a more touching example, small toys have appeared on the tiny graves as if from nowhere. The "Lost Cemetery," as I was told, was definitely a place that would make you jumpy if you walked through it at night. Things dart about in the dark here and then disappear before you can get close to them. Even the moonlit shadows cast by the tree branches seem to have a life of their own.

After the tour I dug deeper into the history of the cemetery and found that it was more than just haunted, but rather, the source of several hauntings. A number of the university's buildings now sit on land once occupied by the Berachah Home. Over the years some of these have come to develop the reputation for being haunted by the ghost of a woman called Mary; a name discovered on one of the tombstones in the lost cemetery. The places said to be haunted by the ghost range from fraternity houses to the university's sandwich shop, but two seem more popular with the ghost than any other. The first is

The grounds that once held the Berachah Home.

the university's Mainstage Theater, where the apparition of a woman is seen dancing around what is commonly known in the business as the backstage "ghost light." This is a light normally left on behind the curtain to allow stagehands to see what they're doing when the theater lights have dimmed. Those encountering the ghost say that she appears in an older, summer dress and bonnet with long, flowing blonde hair. She doesn't seem to care for an audience though, and vanishes after a few seconds. The second hotbed of activity linked to the ghosts of the graveyard takes place in the Student Publications Building. Numerous witnesses have seen the ghost of a little girl they also call Mary wandering the building at night. On one occasion her apparition was even recorded on the security monitors as she floated through the front reception room. At other times certain parts of the building become bone chillingly cold when she is present.

To further the sinister character of the "Lost Cemetery," the body of a young woman was found some years ago on the property. The nature of the tragedy is still uncertain, but the coroner's report lists the official cause of death as exposure. What brought her to the cemetery that cold winter night is still something of a mystery, but some think that she may have fallen asleep and died of hypothermia.

There is something morose about standing in a place where so many have died before they even had a chance to live. But make no mistake about it, the "Lost Cemetery of Infants" is a place of movement and shadow, where certain sounds are hard to explain and you never feel alone. The burial grounds have stood now for over a hundred years and although they seem lost to many they're easy to find if you know how to look.

The "Lost Cemetery of Infants" is located in the northwest corner of Doug Russell Park, 801 West Mitchell Street, Arlington, Texas 76013

The Strange Case of the Glowing Tombstone

...the marker is still there, still glowing faintly rain or snow, moon or moonless. - O. K. Carter, reporter for the *Fort Worth Star-Telegram*

Not far from Carter ghost town, down the same series of convoluted back roads that lie northwest of Fort Worth, sits a quiet, country cemetery with something of a story to tell. Veal Station Cemetery rests safely behind a chain-linked fence, off a narrow black-topped road, four miles from the settlement of Springtown. Legend has it that when the sun drops below the hills, a solitary tombstone within the burial grounds begins glowing in an eerie greenish light. The phenomenon is consistent, night after night, regardless of the weather or any other conditions that might affect it. Because of the secluded nature of the location there are no lights to reflect off its surface or account for the illumination. In fact, it looks much the same as all the rest of the tombstones in the cemetery during the day. For those brave enough to make the trek through clumps of Red Oak and Texas Ash to the marker fifty yards in, another surprise awaits them. Easily seen from the road, the light fades the closer they get to it until the headstone looks confusingly like any of the others. Once lured into the cemetery depths, however, stories tell of a spectral

The gates of Veal Station Cemetery.

woman in white that rises from the earth and chases the violators out screaming in terror.

That's the gist of the story anyway, often claimed as gospel truth from a friend of a friend's second cousin's brother who saw it with their own eyes. Finding an actual firsthand witness, however, proves to be a little trickier. Despite this, the tale evolved into a regular rite of initiation for local teenagers, in a test that required the youth to touch the haunted stone and scamper back before being eaten alive by the ravenous apparition in white. Local newspapers also capitalized on the frightful legend, featuring the story each Halloween in order to thrill readers. This small town story would have remained just that if it hadn't found its way into the wonderful book by Olyve Hallmark Abbott entitled *Ghosts in the Graveyard: Texas Cemetery Tales*. Olyve visited the location numerous times with the help of a local guide, photographing the tombstone, and witnessing the strange glow for herself.

The first settlers to the area founded the small town of Veal Station in the early 1850s. Originally the settlement was known as Creamland or Cream Hill before being named after one of its first citizens, William G. Veal. At the time hostile Indian tribes roamed the land threatening the safety of the tiny community. In response, the town erected a huge bronze bell atop the local Masonic Hall to be sounded whenever the Indians approached. Tensions continued, with the occasional bloody skirmish, until the late 1870s, when the Indians ceased to pose a threat and Veal Station began to assert itself as an important farming center. The town could now boast its own mail service, shops, three churches, cotton and gin mills, and Parson's College with over 500 students. After the railroad bypassed the community, it lost much of its advantage and the population dwindled until nothing remained but a historical marker in 1936. Now the only thing still bearing the name is the cemetery.

When I arrived at Veal Station the summer sun was high overhead and blazing down with all the heat a Texas day could muster. I came early in the hopes of exploring the site and finding the legendary marker while there was still daylight. All I had to go on was a vague description and the photograph of a headstone that looked dauntingly like all the others in the cemetery. While wandering through the burial lanes I happened to notice a man leaning against the trunk of an old ash tree, periodically spitting tobacco juice into an empty beer can. The shadows of the tree gave his gaunt frame and deep set eyes an uncomfortably cadaverous look and I couldn't help but imagine him as some creepy gravedigger out of a 1950s horror film. To head off any suspicions he might be having about my intentions, I gradually worked my way in his direction. I didn't want anyone mistaking me for a vandal - or worse. When I reached his position near the tree I smiled and introduced myself, hoping that an explanation for my presence might ease his mind a bit. I was also hoping I might have found my first-hand witness to the phenomenon of the glowing tombstone. He was however, anything but helpful and insisted that a "fella like me" was wasting my time with such "nonsense."

"Why there ain't no such thing round here," he spit into his can. "The only thing that makes that stone shine is the light atop my dairy barn over yonder."

Usually, encountering a creepy character hanging out in a cemetery for no apparent reason is a good indication that it's time to go, which I did, after thanking him for his advice. I was far from finished, however, and headed back to Springtown to enjoy a few slices at Checker's Pizzeria until the sun went down. While waiting I passed the time with the owner, Debra Steinfels, listening to her stories about the cemetery. Alas, as thrilling as they were, once again they were limited to what she had heard from others.

After the sun had set things finally got dark enough for a "proper" ghost hunt and I headed back to the scene, where I parked my car outside the open cemetery gates. The sounds of the cicadas filled the trees and the heat of the day still lingered in the air. Even from the road, however, it didn't take long to spot the haunting glow of the tombstone across the nocturnal cemetery grounds. There it was, blazing away in ghostly iridescence, just as the stories said it would. This despite the fact that there was no discernable light sources to credit the glow too. Through careful planning I had chosen a night when there would be no moon in the sky. In addition, there were also no streetlights in the vicinity and there certainly wasn't a dairy barn within view. Truth be told, the only source of illumination was a small flashlight I carried with me, whose beam barely made a dent in the darkness. Half the legend was true anyway. The tombstone did glow at night. Now there was only one thing left to do—I had to touch it.

Gingerly stepping across the invisible line that marked the boundary between the haunted burial grounds and the road, I was still a little gun shy after my last encounter in a cemetery alone. One embarrassment was enough and I didn't desire a repeat performance. Setting off along the path, I wound my way through the darker shapes of trees noticing that the closer my steps brought me to the marker, the dimmer it became. By the time I reached what at first I thought was the glowing stone, its unearthly light had faded altogether. Placing my hand atop the flat granite face, I waited. Nothing happened—no spectral lady in white rose from the soil to chase me down, no running or screaming for dear life. Instead, there was just the night, the sound of the insects, and the stifling Texas heat.

Grudgingly I patted its hard surface one last time and turned back to the path that would lead me to the front gate. It was time to call this one and go home. I had faced the legend of the glowing tombstone and...that's when it happened. Traveling along the inky lane I suddenly felt an intense sensation of bitter coldness slam against me, stopping me in my tracks. The air was heavy with an electric quality, causing the hair on my neck to stand on end. I knew I wasn't alone anymore. Someone else was here too and they were watching me, just as the stranger under the tree had been earlier. Scanning the darkness with my flashlight I found no one. As the cold sensation quickly dissipated, I hurried back in the direc-

The glowing tombstone.

tion of my car. With every few steps I turned and looked over my shoulder to make sure I wasn't being followed. The bravado I felt in touching the haunted tombstone moments ago was now gone, replaced with a curious blend of exciting unease. I knew that the events of this evening was something I would not soon forget.

The glowing tombstone indeed turned out to be a rather strange case. The literature involving glowing tombstones abounds with many supernatural tales, yet I couldn't help but think the answer lay in a much more mundane explanation. Our visual perceptions can be less than perfect in conditions that afford very little light. When the eye receives only small amounts of light the number of photons in the human retina decreases. This in turn gives images a blue or greenish tinge. With just the right factors, including poor illumination, distance of the object from the viewer, and the reflective quality of the headstone, it's easy to see how an optical illusion can turn into a haunted tombstone. It also explained why the glow diminishes the closer I got to it. Change any one of these factors even a little and you have just another ordinary tombstone.

What seemed far less ordinary however was the force of bitter cold that stole over me that hot summer night. In the annals of paranormal research, cold spots, or extreme variations in temperature are thought to mark the presence of spirit activity. Ghosts, while attempting to manifest themselves, are believed to draw energy from the environment around them, leaving an intense coldness in their wake. Ghost hunters often seek these cold spots out during investigations as proof of paranormal activity, almost like crime scene investigators look for footprints at the scene of a crime.

Whether or not you find the story of Veal Station Cemetery an amusing bit of local lore or proof positive that ghosts exist, the legend will no doubt continue to thrill many. If you happen to find yourself traveling down an old country road next to a cemetery at night, keep a sharp eye out for an eerie glow. If you spot it through the tree line, approach it with caution, there just might be something waiting for you there. Perhaps something does linger here, waiting for the sound of living footsteps through the soft grass, curious as to what would possess a person to wander through a graveyard alone at night.

Veal Station Cemetery is located four miles south on Highway 51 from Springtown, then turn west for one mile along Veal Station Road.

Interview with a "Cowtown" Ghost Hunter

During the formation of this book I met a host of people involved in the ghost hunting movement who were gracious enough to share with me their time, expertise, and stories. One of those fine individuals included Carl Hullett, a prominent ghost hunter in Fort Worth, who has investigated haunted locations throughout the northern Texas area for years. Carl took time from his busy schedule to sit down with me and share a little about himself and his experiences ghost hunting in Fort Worth. Although people come to ghost hunting with their own story, we each share a bond in that we are all looking for the same answers. The following is the story of Carl Hullett, but it may as well be anyone of us.

Q: Carl, how did you first become involved in ghost hunting?

A: Well, it all began when I was a kid living in Grande Prairie. I was always scared of that house because I thought there was a man living in our attic. I would hear footsteps pacing the attic floorboards and there were a couple of times I even saw him. I began throwing my lunch bag into the attic and coming back later to see if any of it had been eaten. Of course none of it was touched. Then one day I was home sick from school; there was something wrong with my feet, I think, because I couldn't walk. My mother and my grandmother thought I just didn't want to go to school and so left the house to drive around the block. I guess they thought I would get scared and come running out after them. Instead, I literally crawled out of the house and was in the front yard when they pulled up. I was that scared of the man in my attic. That's what really got me believing in ghosts. Years later I met some friends who were into ghost hunting and it peaked my interest. They invited me out to Carter ghost town so I bought a little throwaway camera, a cheap flashlight, and away I went. I had a good time. I had a few experiences too.

Q: What kind of things did you experience at Carter ghost town?

A: There were a lot of shadowy things moving around out there and I got some pictures of orbs, which I later learned that most of it was dust; only a small amount is paranormal. I was in the beginning stages of learning what is and isn't paranormal, but I enjoyed it and they invited me into their group.

Q: What was the name of that group?

A: That was DFW Paranormal Research. We went out every free night we had. Sometimes we would just get in the car and drive around until we found a cemetery and say, " this looks like a good spot." Eventually Les Ramesdale and I veered off from the others and formed DFW Paranormal Research of North Texas. We kept going out as much as possible. We went to places like Bird's Fort and even as far as Hot Springs, Arkansas to an abandoned high school. It was President Clinton's old high school and we had a lot of stuff happen there.

It was about the middle of the night and walking up a flight of stairs we heard what sounded like a man cursing and throwing a wooden board of some kind. We couldn't find anyone even though we locked ourselves in and searched the place pretty well. We even checked outside and, though we kept hearing voices, we never did find anyone.

Q: When did you start the ghost-hunting group DFW Ghost Hunters?

A: It was about four years ago. I picked up a number of other members and we tried to be a little more scientific in our approach. We wanted to know if it was really paranormal or just urban legends. One of our first experiences was at Goshen Cemetery. I didn't really think orbs were anything more than dust particles at the time, until I saw one that night out of my peripheral vision. I was amazed and took a picture as quickly as I could. I told Les about it, but he said you couldn't see one with your naked eye. So we looked at the picture together and sure enough there it was, shining as bright as could be.

Q: What do you think of the modern day ghost hunting movement?

A: Ghost hunting has been around for a very long time, regardless of the fact that we're raised to think that such things aren't real. It's grown a lot in the last ten years. People are starting to get out and experience it for themselves. Once they do they usually want to join a group or even start one of their own. I think we're a long way off from proving anything scientifically, but a lot of people are having their own experiences on a more personal level.

Q: What kinds of people are normally drawn to ghost hunting?

A: People from all walks of life really: the rich and the poor, men and women. People love ghost hunting. Some get a thrill out of being scared. Others have had past encounters. I've heard a lot of people say they lived in a house at one time, where the lights went on and off by themselves or doors would slam shut. Ghost hunting shows on television have also done a lot to get people interested in ghost hunting.

Q: What do you believe ghosts are?

A: I think they can be a lot of different things. Most of the time I think it's just a spirit coming back to say their last goodbyes, or who have a hard time accepting that they're really dead and so won't pass on to wherever it is we're supposed to go. Other times it seems like energy stuck in a place we call haunted; usually where some trauma has happened. There's a lot we don't know about energy. They say energy can never be destroyed, only transformed. If that's the case it has to go somewhere. Maybe sometimes it gets stuck here in the middle and cannot pass on.

Q: What type of equipment do you find useful on investigations?

A: I often rely on electromagnetic field meters (EMF meters). Also temperature gauges, because when something paranormal occurs it sometimes gets colder; on rare occasions it can even get hotter. I also use infrared cameras, regular disposable cameras, digital and 35 mm. I've never really cared for dowsing rods because you can mistake pockets of water or mineral deposits for something paranormal. My favorite, however, is the tape recorder because sometimes you can pick up noises beyond your hearing.

Q: What has been the greatest piece of evidence you have uncovered so far supporting the existence of ghosts?

A: I believe it's something I saw with my own eyes. One time I was doing an investigation in a haunted house when my tape recorder stopped, rewound itself, and began playing from the beginning.

Q: What do you consider the most haunted place you've investigated in Fort Worth?

A: That's a hard one—I would have to say Carter ghost town, because I've had so many experiences there; "Death's Crossing" also.

Q: In your experience what is the scariest encounter you've had on a ghost hunt?

A: I would have to say it was an old abandoned nursing home here in Fort Worth. There were three of us, all big guys, and we were trying to find the dining room. It was said that you could see blood on the tables and you could hear screams. Well sure enough we get back there and there isn't any blood. We did see what we thought were lights and suddenly heard this blood-curdling scream. I tell you what—three grown men came running out of there pretty fast.

Q: Can you tell me about some of the dangers involved in ghost hunting?

A: There can be a lot of dangers depending on the location. I've been in a lot of buildings that looked like they were about ready to fall down on me. You never know, in some old places you could fall right through the floor. There are also other things like snakes, homeless people, or even wild animals that you should beware of.

Q: Carl, before we go, what is the best piece of advice you could give to someone interested in becoming involved in ghost hunting?

A: There are many places where you can contact ghost hunting groups or even just start one yourself. I don't ever recommend you try it alone though. It's not hard to ghost hunt. When I started, all I had was a flashlight, a disposable camera, and a few buddies willing to go with me. There are also a lot of web sites that you can check out to learn more about ghost hunting techniques and haunted locations in your area that are safe to investigate. You can also start writing ghost groups in your area. They usually have a lot they can teach you.

More Ghost Lore: Where to Go

Suggested Readings:

The following is a list of books and articles on the topic of ghosts that you may find helpful to further your understanding of the subject. To list all the material worthy of mention is too big a task for this humble book, however those provided below should give you a good head start.

In General:

Apparitions by G. N. M. Tyrrell

Apparitions and Ghosts by Andrew MacKenzie

Apparitions and Survival of Death by Raymond Bayless

Complete Idiot's Guide to Ghosts and Hauntings by Tom Ogden

Encyclopedia of Ghosts and Spirits by Rosemary Ellen Guiley

The Ghost Hunter's Guidebook by Troy Taylor

Real Ghosts, Restless Spirits, and Haunted Minds by Brad Steiger

True Hauntings: Spirits with a Special Purpose by Hazel Denning

On Texas:

Best Tales of Texas Ghosts by Docia Schultz Williams

Ghosts in the Graveyard: Texas Cemetery Tales by Olyve
    Hallmark Abbott
Ghosts of North Texas by Mitchel Whitington
Ghost Stories of Texas by Jo-Anne Christensen
Ghost Stories of Texas by Ed Seyers
Phantoms of the Plains by Docia Schultz Williams
Spirits of Texas by Vallie Fletcher Taylor
*A Texas Guide to Haunted Restaurants, Taverns and
    Inns* by Robert & Anne Wlodarski
Texas Haunted Forts by Elaine Coleman

Local Ghost Groups and Related Web Sites

Next is a list of local ghost hunting groups in the
Fort Worth area. Their web sites contain a wealth of
information on some of the haunted places that they
have investigated. In addition, many include paranormal
photographs; articles on ghost hunting techniques, and
contact information. All of the groups listed below are
open to investigation requests and new members. If you're
considering becoming involved in ghost hunting, there is
no better way to be introduced to the field than through
a group of experienced ghost hunters. They'll keep you
from making some of the same mistakes that I made.

**Association for the Study of Unexplained
Phenomenon**: www.asup-texas.com
Dagulf's Ghost: www.dagulfsghost.com
DFW Ghost Hunters: www.dfwghosthunters.com
DFW Paranormal Research of North Texas:
www.dfwparanormalresearch.com

Metroplex Paranormal Investigations:
www.metroplexparanormalinvestigations.com
Paranormal Investigations of North Texas:
www.hauntedtexasonline.com
Tarrant County Investigations of the Paranormal:
www.tarrantcountyparanormal.com
Texas Paranormal Research Team: www.tprt.org
Shadow Lands: www.shadowlands.net (Although
not a ghost hunting group, this web site provides an
excellent index of haunted locations in both Texas and
the continental United States.)

Tours In and Around Fort Worth

There are two noted tour operators in Fort Worth
that specializes in haunted tours for the public. Both
are an excellent means to introduce you to some of
the locations around the city and learn more about its
ghostly history.

DFW Ghost Hunters provides guided tours of such
spooky locales as "Death's Crossing" and Carter ghost
town as well as many more in the area. Admission is
$20 a head and in addition to learning the history and
legends of the sites, these ghost hunters show you how
to use the latest ghost hunting equipment and let you
conduct your very own investigation. Booking information can be found on their web site at http://www.
dfwghosthunters.com.

Terri Robinson of Ghost Tours in the Fort Worth
Stockyards leads weekly tours through Fort Worth's
cattle district, exploring such places as Miss Molly's

and the Stockyard's Hotel. Price of admission is $15 and reservations are required. You can book your tour by contacting Terri Robinson at tedwards@dallasnews. com or 817-847-8435.

Paranormal Talk Radio

In our fast paced society of on-the-go news, a number of radio talk shows have surfaced that focus on the paranormal. The programs listed below can be found on both the Internet and radio by visiting their web sites and checking show times. Many of these include a wide range of formats, from interviews with leading experts in the field to lively discussions with listeners who call in.

A.P.S.R. Talk Radio: www.apsrradio.com
Darkness on the Edge of Town Radio Show: www.darknessradio.com
Ghost Talk Radio: www.ghostlytalk.com
Landzedge Radio: www.landzedge.com
Night Watch Radio: www.nightwtachshow.com

Commercial Haunted Houses

For a different kind of fright, you might want to check out some of these local haunted houses during the Halloween season. They've come a long way since I was a kid and many put on major productions involving hundreds of costumed actors and the latest in special effects technology. In addition, many donate part or all of their proceeds to local charities. Traditionally these haunted houses open from the end of September to Halloween night and it may be necessary to check their web sites for times and dates as well as admission fees and directions.

· **The Boneyard Haunted House** is 50 scenes of bone chilling horror, music, food, and games. It's located just south of Six Flags over Texas on Highway 360. Proceeds benefit local Special Olympic Teams. www.theboneyard.org

· **The Chaos Haunted House** is over two acres of terror, music, food, and games. It's located at the Festival Mall off Highway 360 between I-30 and I-20. Proceeds benefit the Advocates for Special People and Special Needs groups within Tarrant County. www.chaoshauntedhouse.com

· **The Cutting Edge Haunted House**—This spooky attraction fills a 235,500 square foot warehouse built in the late 1920s. It's located in downtown Fort Worth at the intersection of I-30, I-35, and Highway 287; these folks really know how to put on a good show. www.cuttingedgehauntedhouse.com

· **The Dungeon of Doom** is nestled in the basement of the Arlington Museum of Art. All proceeds from this haunted house go to support the Museum of Art's children's art education programs. The museum can be found at 201 Main Street in downtown Arlington. www.dungeonofdoomtexas.com

· **Fright Fest at Six Flags over Texas**—An entire amusement park with a Halloween theme. Who could ask for more? It's located at the intersection of I-30 and

Highway 360, twenty minutes from downtown Fort Worth. www.sixflags.com

· **Hangman's House of Horror**—This haunted house celebrates its 18th year of scaring people silly and boasts that it has entertained over 400,000 patrons and donated approximately $1.3 million to local charities. It's located at I-30 and Forrest Park Boulevard in the heart of the city. www.hangmans.com

· **13th Street Morgue** is a haunted theme park combining three attractions in one, including the 13th Street Morgue, Uncle Stinky's Playhouse, and Reindeer Manor. The park can be found at 410 Houston School Road, Red Oak. www.13thstreetmorgue.com

Glossary

Included is a list of terms that every ghost hunter should be familiar with. This is only a brief overview of the ghost-hunting repertoire and is even further narrowed to those found in this book.

Anomaly. Comes from the Greek work *anomalia*, meaning something unnatural or unusual. Anomalies refer to anything strange, appearing on film, sound recordings, or any other unexplained evidence gathered on an investigation.

Apparition. The unexpected appearance of a person, animal, or object in the form of a ghost, phantom, specter, or wraith; the word originated in the Middle English *apparicioun*, meaning to appear.

Dowsing or divining rods. Devices used to search for underground water and mineral deposits as well as the presence of ghosts. These often take the form of bent, hazel twigs, metal rods, or even pendulums.

Earthbound. Describes a spirit or soul trapped on the material plane in the form of an apparition, ghost, phantom, specter, or wraith. This usually occurs near the place of their death or some other familiar location. The reasons for a spirit becoming earthbound are varied and complicated.

Ghost. The soul or spirit of a dead person returned to haunt a location. The word originates from the Middle English term *gost*, meaning spirit or breath.

Haunting. To visit, appear, or inhabit in the form of an apparition or ghost. Hauntings are usually confined to a specific location and for an extended period of time that may even cover hundreds of years.

Hot spot. A location frequented by paranormal activity such as cold spots, orbs, ghosts, etc.

Manifestation. The attempt by a spirit or ghost to materialize itself or influence objects in the material world. This can include cold spots, disembodied voices, apparitions, or the movement of objects.

Medium. A person with the ability or talent to communicate with the spirits of the dead; also known as psychics or "sensatives", the term initially meant "one who stands in the middle ground."

Orb. A sphere or globe of energy created by a spirit that may appear on film or digital images, but remains unseen in most cases to the naked eye. Dust, pollen, water vapor, and insects are know to produce the same effects and are designated as environmental orbs.

Paranormal or supernatural. Events that are beyond what is considered a normal experience or which defy scientific explanation.

Phenomenon. An observable fact, occurrence or circumstance.

Séance. Describes the attempt by a group of individuals to contact spirits of the dead. Normally, a séance is led by one or more mediums that help channel the spirits. The term comes from the Old French, *seoir*, meaning simply – to sit.

Soul or spirit. Both terms are used interchangeably in the text and describe the immaterial, life essence or personality center of each individual.

Urban myths. Modern stories or legends passed on from person to person, often changing with each telling. Although the origins of most urban myths are obscure and contain little supporting evidence, many are found to have some grain of truth to them.

Bibliography

Abbott, Olyve Hallmark. *Ghosts in the Graveyard: Texas Cemetery Tales*. Plano, Texas: Republic of Texas Press, 2002.

Barksdale, E. C. *The Meat Packers Come to Texas*. Austin, Texas: University of Texas, 1959.

Bowen, Elizabeth. *The Second Ghost Book*, edited by Cynthia Asquith. James Barrie, 1959.

Canseler, Norma Todd. *Armstrong's of the Catawaba*. Dallas, Texas: B & W Print and Letter Service, 1969

Carter, O. K. "These ghost stories have a Texas twist." *Fort Worth Star-Telegram*, Oct 17, 2005.

Chapman, Art. "Actors will stand in for the ghosts of historic Fort Worth." *Fort Worth Star-Telegram*, Oct. 7, 2006.

Coleman, Elaine. *Texas' Haunted Forts.* Plano, Texas: Republic of Texas Press, 2001.

Dickens, Charles. *The Haunted House*. New York, New York: Modern Library, 2004.

Douglas MacArthur, "Speech before the joint session of Congress." April 19, 1951.

Eliot, T. S. "To Walter de la Mare." *Collected Poems 1909-1962*. New York, New York: Harcourt, Brace & Co., 1962.

Fitzgerald, F. Scott. *This Side of Paradise*. New York, New York: Reader's Digest Association, 2003.

Garrett, Kathryn. *Fort Worth: A Frontier Triumph*. Austin, Texas: Encino, 2005.

Grieser, Andy. "Ghost of a chance." *Fort Worth Star-Telegram*, Oct. 28, 1995.

"The haunting of Thistle Hill: The case of the ghost hunters and the rocking chair." *Fort Worth Star-Telegram*, Oct 24, 1997.

Guinn, Jeff. "A step-by-step encounter of another kind." *Fort Worth Star-Telegram*, Oct. 31, 1992.

Holland, Gustavus Adolphus. *History of Parker County and the Double Log Cabin*. Weatherford, Texas: Herald, 1931.

Holy Bible: New International Version. Grand Rapids, Michigan: Zondervan Bible Publisher, 1973.

Kennedy, Bud. "Building's ghosts manage to keep business at bay." *Fort Worth Star-Telegram*, Oct 31, 1996.

"Hunting for Haunts: Paranormal investigators check out downtown building." *Fort Worth Star-Telegram*, Oct. 15, 2006.

Knight, Oliver. *Fort Worth, Outpost on the Trinity*. Norman, Oklahoma: University of Oklahoma Press, 1953.

John Malkovich (U.S. stage and screen actor), interviewed by reporter for *The Independent,* April 5, 1992.

Pate, J'Nell. *Livestock Legacy: The Fort Worth Stockyards, 1887-1987*. College Station, Texas: Texas A & M University Press, 1988.

Peter Brothers Hats Homepage, March 8, 2007, www.peterbros.com.

Prather, H. Bryant. *Gleamings of the West*. Weatherford, Texas: Trumpet Publications, 1969.

Rogers, Mary. "Encounters with 'Mattie,' ghost of Mistletoe Heights." *Fort Worth Star-Telegram*, Aug. 21, 1991.

"Ghost encounters of the chilling kind." *Fort Worth Star-Telegram*, October 31, 1993.

"Ghostly visitations downtown." *Fort Worth Star-Telegram*, March 21, 1991.

"Screaming Bridge." *Fort Worth Star-Telegram*, July 10, 1988.

Selcer, Richard. *Hell's Half Acre: The Life and Legend of a Red Light District*. Fort Worth, Texas: Texas Christian University Press, 1991.

Shakespeare, William. *As You Like It*. New York, New York: Oxford University Press, 1994.

Stephens, Anna S. "The Old Apple Tree." *The American Female Poets: with Biographical and Critical Notices*, edited by Caroline May. Philadelphia, Pennsylvania: Lindsay & Blakiston, 1853.

Stevens, Liz. "The lady of the log cabin village…and other spirited tales from Cowtown's Crypt." *Fort Worth Star-Telegram*, Oct 31, 2004.

Whittington, Mitchel. *Ghosts of North Texas*. Plano, Texas: Republic of Texas Press, 2002.

Williams, Docia Schultz. *Best Tales of Texas Ghosts*. Plano, Texas: Republic of Texas Press, 1998.

Phantoms of the Plains. Plano, Texas: Republic of Texas Press, 1996.

Wlodarski, Robert & Anne. *Texas Guide to Haunted Restaurants, Taverns and Inns*. Plano, Texas: Republic of Texas Press, 2001.